MAY 3 1993

Coping with Suicide

A RESOURCE BOOK FOR TEENAGERS AND YOUNG ADULTS

Judie Smith

THE ROSEN PUBLISHING GROUP, INC./NEW YORK

Published in 1986, 1990 by The Rosen Publishing Group, Inc.
29 East 21st Street, New York, NY 10010

Revised Edition 1990

Library of Congress Cataloging in Publication Data

Smith, Judie.
  Coping with suicide.

  (Coping)
  Bibliography: p. 206.
  Includes index.
  Summary: A discussion of teenage suicide, the reasons, the warning signs, the importance of communicating feelings, and the ways the survivors deal with grief.
    1. Youth United States—Suicidal behavior.
2. Suicide—United States—Psychological aspects.
3. Suicide—United States—Prevention. [I. Suicide]
I. Title. [DNLM: 1. Adaption, Psychological—in adolescence—popular works. 2. Suicide—in adolescence—popular works. 3. Suicide—prevention & control—popular works. HV 6546 S653c]
HV6546.S57 1986   362.2   86–10076
ISBN 0–8239–1052–0

Manufactured in the United States of America

ABOUT THE AUTHOR ◇

Judie Smith is recognized as a leading expert on teenage suicide. She has dedicated much of her professional career to the understanding and prevention of suicide. Mrs. Smith holds a BA degree in Psychology from DePauw University and an MA degree in Child Development and Welfare from the University of Minnesota. She continued her studies in Counseling at East Texas State University and the University of North Texas and has received licensure as a professional counselor from the State of Texas.

Judie Smith taught Developmental Psychology in the Dallas County Junior College District prior to joining the professional staff at the Suicide and Crisis Center in Dallas in 1981. She served as Director of Crisis Services, Program Director, Director of Community Services, and Director of Educational Services. In those capacities she was responsible for the training and supervision of crisis counselors, facilitating support groups for survivors of suicide, and conducting seminars on crisis intervention and suicide prevention for the community.

She currently works for the Dallas Independent School District in the Psychological/Social Services Department as a specialist with the crisis team. She helped design and implement the comprehensive suicide prevention project for the District. She is the author of a curriculum on suicide prevention for high school students that is being taught

in schools throughout the country. She conducts training workshops on crisis intervention and grief counseling for school counselors and other mental health professionals.

She has appeared on "The Phil Donahue Show," "Nightline," "The McNeil/Lehrer Report," and the CBS "Morning News." She has testified before the U.S. House Select Committee on Children, Youth, and Families, the Department of Health and Human Services, and state legislative committees on the subject of teenage suicide. She serves as a member of the Texas Education Agency's Suicide Prevention Task Force and is Cochairman of the American Association of Suicidology School Suicide Prevention Committee.

Acknowledgments

I would like to dedicate this book to the volunteers and staff of The Suicide and Crisis Center in Dallas, Texas. Thousands of people have been helped by their efforts and counseling skills. The philosophy and ideas expressed in these chapters reflect those of The Center.

I wish to express my appreciation to the friends and colleagues who have given me encouragement and support during the writing and rewriting of these concepts.

Foreword

Suicide is claiming the lives of more teenagers and young adults than ever before. The tragedy of self-inflicted death reaches far beyond the ultimate death of an adolescent. Parents, siblings, friends, teachers, even entire communities, are often devastated by this ultimate rejection. Until recently suicide was a taboo subject shrouded in secrecy and denial. We can no longer afford to deny realities of suicide.

Coping with Suicide recognizes that teenagers, even more than parents or teachers, are often the first to know when a friend is deeply troubled and at risk for suicide. Judie Smith tells them honestly and clearly how to recognize the warning signs of a suicidal emergency, how to provide emotional first aid, and where and how to get professional help. Her summary of crisis intervention strategies provides the reader with invaluable guidelines for helping a troubled friend.

Coping with Suicide presents troubling and complex information in a straightforward and highly readable manner. Of particular interest is the chapter on surviving the loss of a friend or family member to suicide. Ms. Smith offers both an explanation of the grief process to suicide survivors as well as concrete suggestions for helping someone else recover from the self-inflicted death of a loved one.

Diane M. Ryerson, ACSW
Director

Adolescent Suicide Awareness
  Program (ASAP)
(South Bergen Mental Health Center, Inc.)
Lyndhurst, N.J.

Co-Chairman
School Programs Committee
American Association of
  Suicidology

Preface

The word *suicide* evokes strong emotions. Many would rather not discuss it. It has been regarded as a taboo word, and most people are not prepared to handle the fear and anxiety aroused by the subject, but it has been avoided too long. In the 1980s suicide is so prevalent among teenagers that few escape the necessity either of responding to a friend or acquaintance who is suicidal or of facing the grief when a classmate has committed suicide. This book invites the reader to examine the issues and deal with the topic directly. It is hoped that the subject will become an acceptable topic for discussion at home, in the classroom, and in the church. The effort to understand and be aware may be a life-saving effort.

The case studies used in this book to illustrate various concepts are composites of real cases. The names have been changed to protect confidentiality. Jeanine's story is used with permission from her parents. It is their hope that readers will understand that her death did not have to be and that troubled youth will seek alternatives to their problems. Suicide is an option, but there are other solutions and there are resources and people who are willing to help.

Contents

P A R T ⋄ I

CASE STUDY

CHAPTER 1

Jeanine's Story, as Told by Her Mother

This introduction to teenage suicide is a story about Jeanine. It was a difficult story for her mother to tell. She showed pictures from a family album as she reminisced, sometimes smiling at the happy memories, sometimes with tears in her eyes at the memories of the more difficult times. The pictures depicted the development of a beautiful young girl who never had the opportunity to fulfill her dreams and the dreams of her parents because her life ended abruptly at the age of seventeen when she committed suicide. These are the words of her mother.

I loved her from the minute I saw her. I remember looking at her and thinking, "This is going to be a woman to contend with." She was such a determined child. Even the set of her jaw reflected her stubborn streak. She was very, very sensitive, but oh so stubborn. She resembled her dad with her blonde curly hair, and they had many of the same characteristics: sensitivity and tenacity. My son, Billy, was more like me. It is hard to talk about Jeanine without talking about her brother because they were always together. If a confrontation would happen, he would back down. I would rather make peace than anything. If I see a real battle coming, I'll sit back and wait for another time. I would rather go around the back way and start over. She could never do that, she could never back down. She was very strong-willed in that aspect of her personality.

Jeanine started school in California. We moved to Tulsa, Oklahoma, the following year. We did not realize it at the time, but she was dyslexic and had a hard time in school as she began to learn to read. She was a very stubborn and determined child, but I don't think she ever had confidence in herself after her very bad experience in the second grade. From then on her school experience was tough, and she went through a series of special programs and special schools for children with learning disabilities. At first I wasn't aware that she was having any particular problems. At that time the Tulsa schools had team teaching, with one lead teacher and several assistants. Jeanine's class would go from room to room for different subjects. I didn't know she was having a lot of problems until I went to the school for a parent conference. One of the teachers said to me that Jeanine was very disobedient and they knew that she could do better. She was just not trying hard enough. I was confused and didn't know what to do. I was always accused of spoiling her, and I admit that I did. I liked her so much. I was always accused of letting her be a brat. So I thought, well, it is not for her own good to let her misbehave in school; if she is misbehaving in school, I'm sure the teachers know best. They did not tell me that they were being very strict with her. I would not have approved of the method that they were using.

She started getting stomachaches and not wanting to go to school. I made her go.

One of the young team teachers just out of college called me up and told me that she did not feel right about what was going on in school. I said "What *is* going on at school?" She told me of some really bad incidents, things they were doing to Jeanine because she was not trying hard enough. They would get her up in class, talk about how she was naughty, how she was lazy and would stare out of the window. She was embarrassed and would cry. She would ask the other children for answers to questions that she didn't know, so the teachers called her a cheater and sat her in a corner of the room so no one could talk to her. They didn't let her go out to recess after lunch or go to music class because she didn't finish her work. I became really angry because I thought that was wrong. This young teacher also thought she was being treated unfairly. I did all the things that a parent shouldn't do. I was furious and created all kinds of trouble at school. They had her tested and noted that her reading skills weren't quite good enough. There was something wrong. So they put her in a remedial reading class. She did not improve.

Her personality began to change a little. Ever since she was a little bitty girl she hated anything out of order in her room. She could change things around but she knew where everything was. It was okay if she did it, but she did not like anyone else moving things in her room. After this school experience she would sit there and not be concerned about the disorder. It was just not like Jeanine to be so apathetic.

By this time she was entering the fifth grade. I thought

something was wrong, really wrong. I thought that the testing was not thorough enough. So I took her to the Tulsa University School where they have a clinic for children with learning disabilities. After the tests they told me that Jeanine was very, very intelligent. She had had three bad, frustrating years. They told me that her comprehension was at the eighth-grade level. Her verbal skills were wonderful, but her coordination was bad. She would reverse things when she read. We transferred her to an inner city school where they had special help for her. In the evenings I also took her first to private tutoring, then to a private school three nights a week. Then we had a summer session. The instructors were great. They showed her shortcuts and methods to compensate. They tried to build up her self-esteem, telling her she wasn't stupid but very smart. Jeanine understood what was happening. They tell me that little girls who have low self-esteem become very quiet and withdrawn. Little boys who have a learning disability become belligerent. Jeanine fit the pattern. She had changed from a determined child to a submissive and docile child—except in certain situations; then there was a point when she simply wouldn't take it anymore. That was still a dominant part of her personality.

The special programs included home assignments. We worked with flash cards to help her reading skills. We did some hand and eye coordination things with balls and other little exercises. She always knew that she had this difficulty and it was a problem for her. I would try to find things that she was good at to praise her and help build up her self-esteem.

For a while in Tulsa we had rented a farm and became country bumpkins. Jeanine was very good with animals. She loved animals. We had lambs, a horse, and chickens. The horse had a foal; that was a very special experience for her. She was still going to the special school, and things were beginning to straighten out. It was the tail end of her problems.

Then we left the farm and went to Southeast Asia for a year. Jeanine was a freshman in the International High School there. They had small classes of fifteen. The teachers were excellent because they wanted to be there. Everyone wanted to be in the International School, and Jeanine loved it. We had the pick of the American teachers. They were very happy to be there and very interested in their job. Jeanine did wonderfully in the school and was working at her grade level. Most people did not realize that she had ever had any problems. She still had to work twice as hard; she always did, but she loved her schoolwork anyway. She grew very tall that year. She was five feet ten, which is okay for an adult, but when you are only fourteen it's awful. She was taller than all the boys, and that didn't help her self-esteem at all. People always thought she was older because she was so tall.

We really moved a great deal. After a year in Southeast Asia we moved to Richardson, Texas. The adjustment to her new school was stressful. She had a few really good friends, two or three of them that she hated to leave. In Texas she made a lot of surface friends but no really good friends. This was her second year in high school. She and her dad did not get along. Their personalities clashed. They couldn't walk into a room and say anything nice to each other. There was just that friction there. They were both stubborn. I would run back and forth and try to make peace. I know now that was the worst thing I could have done, but at the time I thought it was what I should be doing.

She was such a sweet girl. She and I hardly ever had words. Unbelievable. She was my best friend. We went everywhere together. She gave me the nicest compliment: She said that all her friends were jealous because we got along like sisters. I was part of the group because I could kid and tease. She used to come in my bedroom with her *Vogue* magazine, and we would sit and talk about clothes and makeup. She would try something new. Her father wasn't a part of any of this; by this time they were really on the outs. This was her sixteenth summer. She didn't get a seventeenth summer.

Jeanine dated a couple of times, but didn't have a steady boyfriend. She never said too much to me about that. She used to say that boys were something for her future and she was more concerned about her career. Of course when we would go out she would joke and make remarks about a "gorgeous hunk." But she said she just had never found anybody that she was that crazy about. She would pay her brother the nicest compliment, saying that she wanted to find a boy just like Billy.

The summer before she died she and Billy, who was now in college, went to Europe together. They rented a Moped and decided to drive around looking for the Loch Ness monster. They never did find it. Jeanine did not drive because of her poor coordination. The two of them fought terribly. Billy had been away at school for four years. Before, when he lived at home, we used to call her his little stooge because she would follow him around and do everything that he did. He was older and she was so impressed. Now when he came home from school she didn't want to do everything that he did. She was growing up. I think toward the end of their trip they had worked it out and had reached an understanding. This was the summer before she died. It was a hard time for her.

Billy came home the Thanksgiving before she took her life. He enjoyed teasing her, and she would squeal with some irritation and annoyance as little sisters do. She loved makeup and would sit in front of her mirror. Billy would sneak up and take her picture and she would squeal. She didn't want him to take her picture while she was putting on her makeup. After she died Billy felt the terrific loss and said he wouldn't come home anymore. He had such a bad time. He hated to see her room, so I packed away her oriental dolls and everything of hers. It helped a lot. Of course we cried as we packed, but it did help because it was like we were making a step forward. We knew that she was gone. We did not want to make her room a shrine because we had been cautioned about that. Billy felt that we might be doing that. Billy was pushing us to do something. He said that we were not healing. So we moved from that house. I guess he was right. It was time to move. Her room was always very sad to me. I would never allow anyone to use it. I kept the door closed and would not let anyone go in. It was just the fear that they would take their lives. It was strange. I still have that fear. I don't trust anyone anymore. I make them promise me all the time that they won't take their lives. It is something that I have to deal with. Not normally, but when we have words of friction and there is tension I make them tell me they won't take their lives. I have to believe them, so I take their word for it. I have to believe them and let it go at that. Sometimes my husband will check it out with me if we have had some tension. We have to do that every once in awhile. Not as much as before, but when there is tension I just don't trust anyone.

Jeanine was under a lot of pressure for a long time, but I did not recognize any of the classic warning signs. She did not give us those signs, although I can see one as I look back. She was staying up late every night and was getting more frustrated with her school work. She was coming up to graduation and staying up to one o'clock or so at night, and I would make her go to bed. I told her she just had to go to bed. Now I can see that that was a lot of tension on her. I can see that as a sign. And she would worry about her weight. This had gone on for a couple of years. She would eat a lot and then worry that she was going to get fat. She would go on these silly diets. I would talk to other mothers and they would say that their daughters worried about the same thing. So I didn't pick it out as something to be concerned about. But combined with all the other things it may have been. I had a son who was under a lot of pressure his senior year. Since he had made it, I thought she could make it. She would come to me and tell me she couldn't make it. I would tell her, "Oh Jeanine, you are so smart, you are so wonderful. I know you can." In a sense I now realize that that was putting even more pressure on her. I didn't realize how to handle it. I could have given her a lot of understanding instead of telling her she was so smart. I have learned.

We were the best of friends. Looking back, I wonder if we really were. She didn't have any best friend here in Texas that I know of. But if I was her best friend, why didn't she tell me? Why didn't she let me know?

She wanted to be an astronomer. She loved the stars and the heavens. She really loved the space program. She started learning about astronomy when she was twelve, and I thought it was a phase that children go through. She was very good in science; it was her favorite. She would read the astronomy magazines and actually understand it all. She did quite all right in math, but her best subject was literature. She could write stories. Any number of teachers told her she should be a writer. She also read a lot of fantasy books. Space and fantasy stories—she loved them. She read a lot of romantic stories about knights and mysticism. Believe it or not, she really liked Shakespeare and the times of kings and queens. She liked the sad stories of Marie Antoinette the best. She identified with how hard it was to grow up.

After she took the SAT exams she wanted to go to UCLA and study astronomy. The school counselor told her that she had better pick another college because she would never make it. She came home that day and cried and cried. Being the defensive mother that I was, I told her that she could take the SAT tests again and take the classes that help you prepare for the test. Jeanine could never take tests well because it took her a long time. She was very smart but she took longer doing the work because she was converting with her eyes. So she didn't finish on time and that reduced her score. I probably did the wrong thing again, but I thought I was encouraging her. She got these results in December and killed herself in January, so she never had the chance to take them again. It was only a month after her counselor had told her she would never make it. That hurt so much.

At school she felt that she didn't fit in. According to the principal and the other kids, she was cheerful and got along with everyone. Everyone liked her but she really had high standards, and a lot of the youths were taking drugs and sleeping around. With our background we did not approve of those things, and she felt really alone. There were not many youngsters who were not getting drunk and taking drugs or sleeping with their boyfriends, so her selection of friends who had the same values was limited. But she did have a couple of friends from church and one girlfriend in particular at school. She really did not have time for outside activities. She would come home and study. She loaded herself down. She had a little job at a toy store in the fall semester of her senior year. We made her quit her job because she would come home at night and study until one in the morning, then get up so early in the morning. We could tell she was under such pressure. She had loaded herself with all these difficult subjects. She had enough credits to graduate after the fall semester of her senior year except for one English course, because the advanced courses at her overseas school were so good. We told her to just breeze through the last semester, take some pressure off. When she came home with the computer read-out of her schedule we said, "Jeanine, why did you do this to yourself?" She said, "I have to take it, I have to, I have to if I want to become an astronomer. It is already in the computer so it's already done." She was seventeen and had made up her mind. I couldn't force her. I didn't think I should force her. Even today I can see that there was no way I could have forced her to change. She had made that decision and had put herself in that pressure spot. She wanted it so badly.

During this time things were not going well with Jeanine and her dad. They didn't like each other. It is as simple as that: They just didn't like each other. My husband and I would have friction over Jeanine. It caused tension between us. Billy could see that they clashed, and he tried to talk to his dad about it, but neither father nor daughter could back down. Jeanine's dad said she was just a smart brat to him and wasn't shaping up. He is the kind of person who is in control. He was standing his ground. She was standing her ground. I was running back and forth and always trying to make everybody happy. You can't do that.

We don't have any close relatives. My mother died before Jeanine was born and my father remarried. He was involved in his own life. My in-laws never really liked me, so they never really liked the kids either. None of them even came to Jeanine's funeral. Isn't that sad? Not one person from her dad's family came to the funeral. I wasn't surprised.

Jeanine had a spat with her best friend the day before she died, which I did not know about. Serena's parents are Jewish. It is my understanding that they believe that suicide is a terrible, terrible sin. Serena took Jeanine's suicide very hard. I have wanted to talk to her about it several times, but her parents were always fluttering around. They did not want us to speak to her about it. They were kind to us. They invited us to dinner but would never leave us alone with Serena or let us talk about it. In fact he would be direct and say, "Don't talk about it." It wasn't until four or five months late that Billy saw Serena, and they discussed Jeanine. Serena said she felt so guilty because the day before Jeanine died they had had a tiff. Even to this day, I wish that I could talk to Serena. Her parents do not wish it, and I will not interfere. Serena is nineteen now, and I worry about it.

Jeanine had another friend that she confided in. We have since talked about Jeanine's suicide. She told me that Jeanine had said she was having a lot of problems. I think this girlfriend felt that she should have done more to help. She is taking it very hard. The week after Jeanine died she eloped with a boy she had known for two weeks. He had a brother who had committed suicide. I think that is why she eloped with him, because he totally understood what she was going through. She was a bishop's daughter. I wonder if Jeanine told her she wanted to die.

In a silly little way I wanted Jeanine's friends around me after she died. I needed them. It was funny. I needed Jeanine's teenage friends. Two of Jeanine's friends from Tulsa, Darcy and Sandra, came down to visit the grave.

Their parents trusted them and trusted me. I felt that Serena's mother and father didn't trust me. It was wonderful that the other parents allowed us to be together without their presence. I think that those two girls from Tulsa have worked through it. On Jeanine's birthday Darcy called me and cried and cried. She said that she thought of Jeanine all the time and how she would have been in college too. It was nice that she did not forget.

I really don't know what Jeanine told her girlfriends. From my curiosity I wanted to know what other pressures Jeanine had. I knew about the school and home. I wish that they could free themselves up and talk more about it.

The night before Jeanine died the family had another argument. My husband was going to Norway in a few days on business. We had all gone to see a movie and were in the car on the way home. Jeanine was sitting in the back seat. I said to my husband, "Since you are going to Norway, how about bringing Jeanine a silver bracelet as a gift." Jeanine, from the back seat said, "Yeh, yeh, yeh." Her dad said, "Do you think I am made of money?" I don't even remember what else was said. It was just arguing. It was a hateful argument. I said, "Oh, you make me feel so guilty. Sometimes I just wish I were dead." It was a ploy on my part, I know that. Jeanine in the back seat was listening all this time, taking all this in. She really wanted a bracelet, and I'm sure that she was disappointed. When I made that remark (it was just a passing remark that you make), from the back seat she said, "I do too." If she had not taken her life the next day, I would not have remembered it. When we got home from the movie nothing more was said. We all went to bed.

The next morning she came into my room and hugged me. We often hugged. We were always hugging. My husband was already up and in the other room. Jeanine crawled into my bed and snuggled next to me and said, "Oh Mommy, you are the best." And I said, "Oh Jeanine, you are the best thing in the whole world." Then she got up and went into the next room and ate and watched television. It was Sunday. We spent the morning just lounging around. Her dad wanted to watch the Superbowl game later in the afternoon, and Jeanine wanted to watch *Camelot*, which was on at the same time. She had seen it before, so he won the argument and she sulked in her room.

While waiting for the game to begin, we started to play a card game, and Jeanine asked if she could play too. She was winning. She never liked to lose. Even in a card game she would get angry if she lost. Since she was winning, we couldn't understand why she was still sulking. It was as if she was dreaming off and we had to remind her when it was her turn to play the cards. A look of anger came over her face like I have never seen before. She stood up and said, "I don't want to play this stupid game." She threw down her cards and went out of the room in a huff. We did not understand that, because she was winning. Her dad kept telling her to play the cards and maybe picked at her a little bit, but we did not know why she got so angry. It was a temper tantrum. We looked at each other and laughed because it was such a childish thing. I remember saying, "Wow, is she in a sniff!" We finished the card game and then the football game started. We sat there for awhile. I thought that since she used to pull tantrums when she was a little girl, it was best to let her go to her room and get it out. It was best to leave her alone and let her have her privacy. I thought she was tired, that she was under a lot of pressure at school and was in a bad mood. We had had that agrument the night before, her dad had felt real bad about it that morning and had offered to take everyone out to dinner, but that didn't really appease her. So I thought that she might still be pouting over the night before.

After about forty-five minutes I thought she had probably calmed down and I had better go in and see how she was. Her door was closed. When I opened the door I found her hanging there. At that point it was like a dream. It was such a shock. I screamed and screamed. She had hanged herself from a curtain rod with an exercise rope. It was like I was in a dream world. I felt shame. It was an intense sense of shame. And then there was a sense of relief. It is okay to say that now. And then I was ashamed of that relief sense. All these feelings that washed over me were unbelievable. I was in a dream world as if it wasn't really happening. Then I had all these other horrible feelings. We got her down and gave her mouth-to-mouth resuscitation. I called the police. But I knew she was dead. Something was missing. I was hoping, but I knew it was only her form left. I don't know how to explain it. There was just something missing.

The police called back because they must have thought it was a prank call. I begged them to come and bring an ambulance. When they came, they took over trying to revive her. They made me leave the room. I kept asking if she was still alive. The police were very, very kind. We followed the ambulance to the hospital. We suspected that she was not going to live, but a corner of our hearts hoped that she would. We were in a crazy daze. I felt nothing for several days. It was like I was not really there. I was numb. I was there. Jeanine was gone.

I always think about these wonderful books that are written about people's tragedies. Shakespeare's tragedies, for example. You read the tragedy and feel sorry for the victim. Then after you understand all the characters you have compassion for all of them. They do the best that they can do. And at the end you realize that no one can be judged because most people are doing the best that they can do. I can see all of our parts in this, but I can also say that we did the best we knew how to do at the time. I know that I overlooked some things, I didn't have knowledge of certain things. I made mistakes. Maybe if I had had that knowledge I could have intervened. But I didn't. I only did the best that I could. And I think we all did. We all failed Jeanine in certain ways, but the prime one to fail was Jeanine. We realize that. We wish that we had done some things differently and we wish that she would have seen a different option, but that is something we can't change now. It took a long time to accept that, and there are still days that we don't. There are days that we are still angry at God, at her, at each other. Sometimes I think we are doing quite all right and other times I think we are not. We don't hit the bottom as low as we used to and we don't stay there as long. I think for the most part we are making a valiant effort to go on.

Jeanine could not handle her imperfections. Both she and her parents set high ideals for her. They did not communicate to her that it was okay for her to fail or to be average. They believed that they made mistakes but are imperfect too. With any relationship there is bound to be hurt and pain along with the love and joy. Often the quest for perfection leads us to be unforgiving. Forgiving is a hard thing to learn. Some people live their whole lives and never learn it. It is called maturity but it has nothing to do with age. Nine months after Jeanine committed suicide, her parents are learning to forgive and ask for forgiveness.

PART ◇ II

UNDER-STANDING THE ISSUES

CHAPTER 2

Some Things to Know about Suicide

A. CHANGING ATTITUDES

Man has been plagued by suicide for thousands of years. History documents the struggle between self-destruction and self-preservation even among the ancient Egyptians. Attitudes toward suicide have changed from society to society and from generation to generation. Primitive man often included suicide as part of a religious ritual or encouraged it as an honorable act following the death of a chieftain. Until the last century in certain parts of India it was customary for widows to commit suttee (suicide) to help atone for the sins of their husband. Hara-kiri (self-disembowelment) also was an honorable death for the nobility and warriors of Japan. During World War II the Japanese kamikaze pilots willingly forfeited their lives to destroy the enemy.

The Bible reports a dramatic story of mass suicide at

Masada when a whole Jewish commuity chose death rather than occupation by the Romans. History repeated itself in Crete as recently as the nineteenth century when thousands of men, women, and children resisted the Turkish invasion of Arkadiou by blowing themselves up in the sanctuary of a monastery. Mass suicide also occurred in contemporary times when hundreds of Americans chose death at the direction of a misguided and deranged cult leader at Jonestown, Guyana.

Other cultures did not view suicide as courageous or honorable but discouraged suicidal behavior with threats of religious censorship and stigma and imposed legal punishments on the survivors. Most of the early Greek philosophers considered suicide cowardly and offensive to the state, although the later philosophers recognized the rational aspect of suicide as an option in the most hopeless circumstances.

Although the Bible neither condones nor condemns suicide, as the frequency of suicide increased during the early centuries, Christianity shifted from the glorification of martyrs to the denial of Christian burial for suicide. The influence of the position of the Catholic Church became evident during the Middle Ages. Suicide was considered a sin against God, and the fear of eternal damnation and the wrath of the Church seemed to deter those who despaired of life from considering wilfully destroying it. The incidence of suicide decreased.

The age of enlightenment and philosophical insight brought a change in attitude toward suicide as man began to accept free choice and to understand human emotions. The scientific study of suicide was introduced by the French sociologist Émile Durkheim with the publication of his scholarly work *Suicide* in 1897. He postulated a theory of suicide that gave rise to the research and clinical efforts at suicide prevention that continue today. His sociological investigation described three basic types of suicide that varied with the amount of social integration, control, and structure: *altruistic, egoistic, and anomic.* Altruistic suicide included the traditional Indian suttee and the self-immolation of the Vietnamese monks protesting the oppression of the government. Egoistic suicide describes those who are alienated from society and are more inward-oriented than bound by religious ties or laws. Those who face an abrupt change in role or identity are categorized by Durkheim as anomic. They question their purpose in life and the essence of their being following a traumatic disruption.

Recent decades have seen dedicated efforts by researchers and clinicians to understand the dynamics and needs of suicidal persons. Whereas suicide was once a taboo subject, we are now encouraging the exploration of attitudes and the acceptance of feelings that lead many to the brink of despair, in hope that empathy and understanding will break the sense of isolation and persuade suicidal persons to seek professional help. Suicide is viewed as a tragedy and generally accepted as preventable.

The topic of suicide can no longer be ignored. It is a major cause of death among young people. We used to believe that suicide was something that happened in someone else's family or another community. We spoke of it in hushed tones so as not to be overheard. Authors used suicide as the ultimate human tragedy for storybook heroes or heroines, but it was not accepted as a real-life occurrence. It was reserved for fiction.

Indeed, suicide is the ultimate human tragedy, but it is not reserved for the novels and movies. It happens to the senior class president and the National Merit Scholar as well as to the quiet kid who didn't have many friends or the eighteen-year-old who has been an alcoholic since he was fourteen.

We cannot afford to treat suicide as a taboo subject. If we are to help those who are struggling with the choice of life or death, it is necessary to learn how to recognize when someone is asking for help, how to respond to that powerful message, and where expert professional counseling is available. It is our belief that the most effective programs to reverse the frightening increase in the rate of teenage suicide must include efforts to teach young people as well as adults the fundamental techniques of crisis intervention. These basic communication skills can arm family and friends with the confidence of knowing something they can do to help someone in crisis. It is similar to the importance of neighborhood crime-watch programs. The police cannot combat crime alone and prevent the burglaries and robberies in every neighborhood. Neighbors are encouraged to watch and help each other by their willingness to become involved. Suicide attempts are a cry for help. If the only ones who know how to recognize and hear that cry are the psychiatrist, the therapist, or the professional crisis counselor, too many of those needing help will go unheard. The painful message of desperation is usually intended to catch the attention of loved ones and friends. That message is frightening to hear. It is even more frightening to hear it and not know what to do or where to turn for help and become immobilized by that fear.

Professional suicidologists now encourage open discussion of suicide. Suicide prevention can begin with surrounding the suicidal person with caring and understanding from supporting family and friends. Ignoring the topic will not make the issue disappear, and open discussion in school will not cause someone to kill himself any more than sex education will increase the rate of teenage pregnancies.

B. TRENDS AND STATISTICS:
THE EXTENT OF THE PROBLEM

We shall begin exploring the issue of suicide by examining the scope and trends of its occurrence. Figures and statistics can be misleading and often inaccurate. The incidence of suicide is probably far underreported. We can get a general idea of the extent of the problem of teenage suicide and how it has increased in recent decades by examining some of the reported statistics. Then we should be aware that these figures represent just the tip of the iceberg.

Over 5,000 young people under the age of 25 commit suicide each year in the United States. The statistics are reported as a rate per 100,000. By using a rate we can compare year by year or city by city, even though there may be changes or differences in population. By using a rate we can understand if there is a real increase or decrease or an unusually high or low incidence of suicide. In 1986, for the age bracket of 15–24, the rate was 13.1 per 100,000. Of all the young people who die, 12.8 percent kill themselves. Suicide is the third leading cause of death for this age group. On the average, one adolescent commits suicide every hour and a half each day. Accidents cause more deaths than suicide, but it is very difficult to know how many one-car accidents are really suicides. For that reason it may be that suicide kills more people than any other cause of death among adolescents and young adults. Periodically the homicide and suicide rates switch places in the vital statistics reports. In some years suicide is the second leading cause of death and homicide is third.

If we look at the high school ages (14–18) we find that the rate per 100,000 was 6.79 over a three-year period between 1982 and 1984. If there are 100,000 teenagers between the ages of 14–18 in a hypothetical community and seven of these children committed suicide, this community has the average amount of high school age suicides.

	Suicide Trends in the United States Ages 15–24				
Year	Total All Groups	White Males	White Females	Black Males	Black Females
1981	5,161	3,775	856	316	71
1980	5,239	3,881	811	346	69
1979	5,246	3,727	875	389	97
1978	5,115	3,689	869	356	76
1977	5,565	4,027	948	349	105
1976	4,747	3,354	839	341	101
1975	4,736	3,378	832	323	86
1974	4,285	3,025	796	274	88
1973	4,098	2,905	706	302	83
1972	3,858	2,540	738	338	114
1971	3,479	2,326	735	214	113
1970	3,128	2,116	649	214	84

Source: Division of Vital Statistics, National Center for Health Statistics, as reported in *Teenage Suicide, The Final Cry.*

More young adults and adolescents commit suicide each year than any other age, but they are not the highest risk group. The risk for suicide increases with age. In 1986 the rate was 21.5 for ages 65 and older. However, the population is smaller, so the actual number is less. Only .4 percent of deaths over the age of 65 are suicides compared to 12.8 percent of adolescent deaths. The elderly made up 12.1 percent of the population in 1986 but committed 20.3

[1] John McIntosh. "Suicide Facts and Myths with a Focus on Age and Sex." Presentation to AAS convention, Toronto, 1985.

percent of the suicides. Sixteen percent of the 1986 population were young, and they committed 16.6 percent of the suicides. (McIntosh)

The suicide rate for young people has tripled since 1955. The increase is due mainly to the increase in the rate for males. Several factors may be at work here: (1) suicide prevention centers have deterred suicide among young females; (2) rescue methods have been improved for drug overdoses, the method preferred by females; and (3) employment has a positive effect on self-esteem and the feeling of personal control over one's life for females. This increasing suicide rate warrants great concern and indicates the need for school suicide prevention programs.

The 1990 health objectives for the nation that were developed by the U.S. Public Service Office of Disease Prevention and Health Promotion states that by 1990 the rate of suicide among people 15–24 should be below 11 per 100,000. When these objectives were written the rate was 12.4, so it seemed to be a realistic hope to reduce the rate by 1.4. At first there was some indication that the rise in rates for young people had peaked in 1977 and would level off, but unfortunately recent statistics do not bear this out. The 1986 rate of 13.1 is even higher than the 12.4 figure we had wanted to reduce.

Males commit suicide three times as often as females. Of the 30,904 suicides in 1986, 24,226 were males and 6,678 were females. For adolescents the difference is even greater: the ratio is almost five male suicides to one female suicide. Boys are more prone to use violent, aggressive methods such as guns or hanging, which are more lethal than the methods of drug overdose or slashing the wrists preferred by girls. Fifty-five percent of all teen suicides are by guns. Although boys use guns more often and thus die more often, girls who do die are more likely to have used a gun than a drug overdose. The availability of the method influences the choice. In New York people throw themselves off tall buildings; in San Francisco the Golden Gate Bridge attracts suicidal jumpers; in Texas, people use guns.

The incidence of suicide is much greater among whites. Over 28,000 of the 30,904 suicides were committed by whites and only 2,467 by nonwhites. The suicide rates are highest in the Western states and lowest in the Middle Atlantic states.

If we focused our attention only on these statistics of completed suicides, however, we would fail to grasp the extent of the problem. Many, many more do not die from that attempt—at least not the first. The rate of suicide attempts, although difficult to substantiate, is calculated as nearly one hundred times the number of completions. Even that calculation may well be an underestimate. Two studies, one in California and one in Kansas,[2] reported that 13 percent and 8.4 percent of the teenagers questioned admitted having made one or more attempts. Ninety percent of those attempts do not come to the attention of medical personnel or police authorities and thus do not find their way into statistical records.

Even more frightening are the reports of how many teenagers seriously consider suicide. Perhaps as much as 40 to 50 percent have at one time been attracted to the notion of suicide to block out the unhappiness that they are experiencing.

Statistics give us some additional facts about suicide. More suicides occur during the daylight hours. The night hours may be lonely for the depressed, but they are likely to make it through the night and act on the decision to end life when the sun is shining.

[2] Kim Smith. Presentation to AAS convention, Toronto, 1985.

In some parts of the country a death is not ruled a suicide unless a suicide note is found as evidence of intention. Sometimes, if a note is written, it is destroyed or hidden by a shamed and embarrassed family, which further complicates the matter. Only 20 to 30 percent of suicides leave a note, but the absence of a note does not indicate that the death was not self-inflicted.

Weather does not seem to affect the suicide rate. There is no greater incidence of suicide on dark rainy days. Nor is there a correlation between the suicide rate and the full moon. Perhaps these beliefs stemmed from associating the act of suicide with gloom, doom, and mystery.

Much is written about the holiday blues and depression that may accompany the experience of loneliness during the Christmas season when family closeness and sharing do not occur. The holiday blues may be real, but the suicide rate does not increase during that time. In fact, the suicide rate increases slightly during April and May. That is surprising, since we think of spring as uplifting and joyful, but perhaps it is the very reason more people kill themselves in the spring. When you are depressed the warm sunshine and balmy breezes are not sufficient to take away the sadness. In addition, the contrast in mood between the depressed person and what seems like everyone else in the world may further deepen the despair.[3]

C. DEFINING SUICIDE

Death may be classified in four ways: natural death, accidental death, homicide, or suicide. Suicide describes the

[3] Kathleen MacMahon, "Short-Term Temporal Cycles in the Frequency of Suicide; United States, 1972–1978." *American Journal of Epidemiology*, Vol. 117, No. 6, 1983.

voluntary and intentional taking of one's own life. Homicide is the taking of another person's life. Accident is a death that is unexpected and unintentional, that occurs by chance. Natural death results from illness or old age. That seems like a simple way to categorize death for the purpose of statistics and research. But nothing about suicide is simple, even its definition. When a coroner, medical examiner, or justice of the peace is called to a death scene, it is often difficult to determine whether the death was self-inflicted and intentional. When the suicide victim communicates the intent and desire to die by leaving a written note, that is strong evidence that the death was self-inflicted and the ruling of suicide is more clear-cut. However, less than 30 percent of those who commit suicide leave a note. It is also not unusual for the family to want the death ruled something other than suicide because of the embarrassment, shame, and legal complications that may arise following a suicide. Evidence may be destroyed or withheld from the authorities. and the suicide ruling becomes difficult.

When the field agent for the medical examiner's office arrived at the house, he found an eight-year-old boy hanging by his belt from the top bunk of a double-decker bed. The boy was dead. He had had an argument with his mother and stormed upstairs, slamming his bedroom door behind him. When he did not come to the table at dinner, his mother checked on him and found his body. The field agent originally ruled it a suicide, but after further investigation that ruling was changed to accidental death. An eight-year-old child does not have the cognitive ability to understand the abstract concept and finality of death. It was decided that the child had no intention of killing himself; therefore it was ruled an accident. Even if young children do not understand the finality of death, we are seeing suicidal behavior in very young children. Perhaps it is not death that is sought, but there is a definite indication that some children think they simply should not exist.

✳There are also different degrees of intentionality. Suicide is generally described as a cry for help. Most often a suicide attempt is an effort to communicate the turmoil and pain and not a real intent to cease consciousness forever. It may be described by some suicidologists as parasuicide or a self-inflicted injury with low lethality. Low lethality means little likelihood that death will be the result, either because there is a chance for intervention or because the means is not lethal, as in a drug overdose or a minor slashing of the wrist.

Susan and her husband had a violent argument before he left for work. He wanted out of the marriage and told her that morning that he was going to move out. She suspected he had another relationship and accused him of having an affair. He denied it but told her it really didn't matter because he had made up his mind that there was no hope of making their marriage work. When the door closed behind him, Susan knew this was not like the other times they had fought and made up. She spent most of the day staring into space or crying. Late that afternoon she tried to rest but found herself so full of anxiety that she was too tense to relax. She took some sleeping pills but still could not sleep. All she wanted was not to have to think about her problems and to find relief from the ache and turmoil she felt. She took some more pills and this time drank a couple of beers, and then lay down on the sofa. She thought that her husband would soon come home to pack up his clothes, and she pictured him finding her and the empty pill bottle and rushing to the hospital with her in his arms. But Jim did not come home that night, and Susan died.

Was this suicide? She took the pills and drank the alcohol

knowing the danger but not fully intending to die. It could logically be considered an accident but under the circumstances would most likely be ruled suicide.

D. THE LEGAL ISSUE

Laws reflect the mores of the society that enacts them. Laws change as attitudes and values change. This is evident throughout history in respect to suicide. Suicide victims and their families have been ostracized, shamed, and legally punished. At one time in England suicide was considered a crime against the king because it deprived the ruler of taxes. The victim was not permitted burial in the church cemetery, and the family property was confiscated to reimburse the king for his loss.

Until the last decades suicide was considered a crime in many U.S. states, although persons who attempted it were rarely brought to trial. Even though suicide is no longer illegal, there is still confusion in some people's minds. It is perfectly clear, however, that the law does not permit aiding in someone else's suicide.

In a recent case in Texas a young man was convicted of helping his roommate commit suicide by buying a gun for him and encouraging him to use it. He was even present when the suicide took place. There was little question in the eyes of the law in that case, but others may not be so clear-cut. A devoted spouse provides drugs for a beloved mate who is dying an agonizing death from cancer. Two lovers make a suicide pact; one dies and the other survives. Is the survivor guilty of aiding in the other's death? These become both legal and ethical issues.

E. RATIONAL SUICIDE

In recent years movements have arisen abroad and in the United States to condone suicide and to support those who are rationally considering killing themselves. EXIT in Great Britain and the Hemlock Society in the United States publish newsletters and books teaching various methods of suicide and describing the act as courageous and logical under certain circumstances. These societies are controversial, and in some instances their publications are banned. There is lively dialogue between those who advocate rational suicide and those who seek to prevent suicide, the differences of opinion stemming from the difficulty in defining rational suicide or in accepting the act of suicide under any circumstances.

Edwin Shneidman, founder of the American Association of Suicidology, believes that there is no such act as rational suicide but that every suicide has its own logic—although most of that logic is flawed. The ironic conclusion is that suicide should never be committed when one is suicidal, for how can anyone be rational when under tremendous stress?

Rational means reasonable. It is assumed that if the correct logical steps are followed in reaching a conclusion, then the mental process is reasonable. But is the conclusion reasonable if the original premise is unacceptable? If the original premise is that the suffering is irreversible, that statement must be a fact to justify the conclusion that suicide is rational. When physical suffering is great, death is imminent and inevitable, and the suffering cannot be alleviated, suicide may be reasonable for some people. But can suicide be considered rational for those whose life has lost meaning and who are grieving after the death of a spouse? In the case of a grieving widow or widower, there is a possibility that the suffering will lessen and the quality of life once again improve to create new meaning. The struggle may be intense, but hope is also a rational possibility.

F. DISPELLING THE MYTHS

Since suicide has not always been an acceptable subject for discussion, untruths and half truths were guessed or repeated without searching for factual information. Even the word *suicide* was so emotion-laden that it was avoided. This was particularly true for those who had had some firsthand experience, yet they were the ones who most needed accurate information. One of the first efforts of those in the field of suicidology was to dispel some of the misinformation that had been handed down from generation to generation.[4]

Myth 1. People who talk about suicide will not commit suicide. This may be said with a sigh of relief: "At least he is getting it off his chest. Now I don't have to worry." How far from the truth that is! People who talk of suicide quite often attempt or even complete suicide. Mentioning suicide should be taken as an indication that something is wrong and should always be taken seriously.

Sandy was married at the age of eighteen. Her new husband, Vic, threatened suicide on their wedding day. They had a minor disagreement, and he said he might as well kill himself if that was how she was going to act. As the years went by he continued to use the threat of suicide to manipulate and scare her into complying with his wishes. It was a powerful means of control over her, and his threats

---

[4] E.S. Shneidman and N.L. Farberow. "Some Facts about Suicide." PHS Publication NR. 852, U.S. Government Printing Office, 1961.

escalated. He bought a gun, kept it close by and loaded. Then he started pointing it at himself when they argued. Sandy gave in and gave in. She recognized the bind she was in but felt helpless to change anything. One night Vic put the loaded gun to his temple as they stood nose-to-nose in the heat of an argument. She looked him square in the eye and said, "Go ahead." He did, right then and there. She was convinced that he did not mean to do it and that it was really an accident. Vic had threatened many times. Whether he meant to or not, he took his own life.

Myth 2. All suicidal people want to die. There are degrees of intentionality. Those who choose a very lethal method without communicating intent are far outnumbered by those who communicate a desperate cry for help and use a suicide gesture to manipulate others. The majority of suicidal people are ambivalent: Part of them wants to die, part of them wants to live. Therein lies the conflict and struggle. A suicidal person may not be consciously aware of his ambivalence.

Tommy drove his car to the emergency room parking lot of a large county hospital. He pulled into a spot close to the entrance that was visible to the guard and all those who entered or exited. Then he shot himself.

Tommy was ambivalent. The part of him that wanted to die was the part that pulled the trigger. The part of him that wanted to live drcve to the hospital first. It was not death he sought, but an escape from life as he knew it. That is an important distinction. The motivator behind the suicide is not the permanent ceasing of existence, but the immediate ceasing of consciousness because it is painful to be conscious.

Myth 3. If you ask someone if he wants to commit suicide you might give him the idea; therefore avoid any such direct questioning. Logical as this may seem, it simply is not true. Bringing the topic into the open will not begin that kind of thought process for someone who is in a crisis. If a person is suicidal, it is not because someone asked if he were considering it. Many people are inhibited from initiating the subject because of their own fears. If you are close to someone, you do not want to hear the answer that he wants to die. It is very frightening to hear the words, "I don't want to live anymore," because we know we will face emptiness and grief upon the death. Since suicide is so difficult to discuss, it is often the case that someone who is thinking about suicide has had no one to talk to about it. If you have the courage to bring up the subject, it may be the beginning of relief from the tension and anxiety that accompany suicidal thoughts.

Myth 4. Suicide happens without warning. This myth may hold a little bit of truth, but studies reveal that over 80 percent of suicidal people do give many clues to their intentions. That leaves only 20 percent who do not communicate their desire to die, and they are more likely to be middle-aged or older and to die with the first attempt. The younger suicidal person is more likely to let others know he is in pain or to manipulate and control others. The elderly are the completers and the teenagers are the attempters. That statement does not mean that teenagers do not die when they attempt, as we are well aware, but it does give us hope that their suicides can be prevented if we learn the warning signs. Professional suicidologists encourage school suicide prevention programs to begin with the classic warning signs. These are discussed in detail in Chapter 4.

Myth 5. Once a person is suicidal, he is suicidal forever. This myth paints a pretty bleak picture of huge numbers of people existing with no hope or happiness in their lives. Recent studies indicate that 10 to 13 percent of teens have attempted suicide one or more times. Perhaps as much as

40 percent have thought about it seriously. It is possible and in fact very probable that someone can find himself in a crisis, consider suicide as an alternative, find another solution, and work through the crisis with an understanding of what it is like to be so afraid, angry, or sad and also learn to welcome the joy and delight that life can offer. Persons who wish to kill themselves are suicidal for a limited period of time. The decision to commit suicide can always be redecided.

Myth 6. Suicide is inherited. The confusing aspect of this myth is that some families have more than one suicide in their history and it does seem to "run in the family." That does not mean that suicidal behavior is predetermined by genetic structure. It does mean that once a suicide occurs in the family, other family members are at higher risk for committing suicide. The suicide victim leaves a legacy that includes permission to choose suicide as an escape from painful experiences in life. Cheryl was haunted by this legacy. Her grandfather, a great-uncle, and a brother died by suicide. Her mother spoke of the family as doomed or cursed and told the children it was their family's fate. Cheryl expected more suicides to happen. She did not realize that suicide is an individual choice. It is not inevitable and passed on from one generation to the next through the genes. Much of our behavior is learned from parents or any family member who is a role model. If grandfather kills himself, that solution becomes more acceptable to others in the family who admired and loved him. Even though the tendency to commit suicide appears in some families, it is not the result of a heredity trait. Often suicide and depression go hand in hand. Suicide itself may not be inherited, but it is quite possible that a predisposition is. There may well be a chemical imbalance that is caused by a genetic abnormality. Chemotherapy may alleviate this imbalance and, coupled with psychotherapy, relieve the depression.

Myth 7. All suicidal people are mentally ill. That, of course, depends on the definition of mental illness. Broadly speaking, mental illness refers to emotional problems, and anyone in a crisis certainly experiences intense emotions. Suicidal thoughts often accompany depression, and when depression interferes with normal daily functioning, it may be serious enough to be classified as a mental disorder.

In a stricter sense, mental illness describes the more severe mental disorders of a psychotic person. A psychosis is characterized by difficulty in dealing with reality and the presence of hallucinations (hearing voices, seeing things that are not there) or delusions (false beliefs such as thinking you are Jesus or Napoleon). The myth that suicide is always the act of a psychotic person arose from the idea that anyone who would seek death must be "crazy." The survival instinct is a strong motivating force in human behavior, and it was believed that if that force was missing or in conflict it must indicate the presence of a mental illness. Not all people who find themselves in a crisis are crazy or need to be in a mental institution. If psychosis is present, however, the risk of suicide increases, particularly in those suffering from schizophrenia (a severe functional psychosis characterized by withdrawal from reality, where the person seems to live in a world of his own) or a manic-depressive psychosis (characterized by extremes of mood, often by wide swings from intense excitement to deep melancholy). Suicidologists who study notes left by suicide victims find that although the suicidal person may have been extremely unhappy, he was not necessarily psychotic.

Myth 8. Suicide occurs exclusively among the poor or the rich. We may think that someone must be destitute to want to die. When the basic necessities of shelter, food, and clothing are not available, we imagine the struggle to exist would be overwhelming and it would be understandable if the person wanted to give up. On the other hand, if money is plentiful and luxuries come easily, why would anyone want to die? Suicide strikes among the rich as well as the poor. It cuts across all socioeconomic levels. Young suicides are found in all families from blue-collar workers to successful professionals. The pain people suffer may be the result of stress and anxiety because the bills can't be paid and the children are hungry, but it is more likely the result of relationship problems.

G. SUMMARY

Suicide has been recorded throughout the history of man. Attitudes toward suicide vary from culture to culture. Some societies have accepted it as honorable and even encouraged it under certain conditions. Other societies abhorred it and imposed religious sanctions or harsh punishment on the survivors. In contemporary society, suicide has been regarded as a taboo subject. We are now encouraging open discussion and examination of personal attitudes, and we tend to view suicide as a preventable tragedy.

Suicide is the third leading cause of death among young people. The rate tripled from 1955 to 1977. In the early 1980s the rate leveled off, and it was hoped that the decreasing trend would continue. More recently, however, the increase has resumed. Suicide is defined as the act of voluntary death. The issue is clouded because it is not always easy to determine whether the death was intentional and the family may not want the official ruling of suicide. Thus, it is not unusual for a suicide to be ruled an accident.

As a result of recent research, new information about suicide is dispelling the old myths. The following statements are TRUE:

1. People who talk about suicide frequently do attempt and commit suicide.
2. Most suicidal people are ambivalent about their death wish.
3. Asking people about suicidal intentions will not cause them to commit suicide.
4. Suicide rarely happens without warning.
5. Once a person is suicidal, he is not necessarily suicidal forever.
6. Suicide is not inherited.
7. Not all suicidal people are crazy.
8. Suicide occurs in both the upper and lower socio-economic classes.

H. DISCUSSION QUESTIONS

1. What are some reasons that people would wish to avoid discussing the subject of suicide?
2. Why are suicide statistics difficult to obtain?
3. What is your attitude toward suicide? Do you view it as morally acceptable, wrong, or is it not a moral issue for you?
4. Can you think of a time when suicide could be considered rational?
5. Why is it difficult to define suicide, and how would you define it?
6. Find out if your state has any laws regarding suicide.
7. Which of the myths that are listed have you heard? Why do you think people believed those myths?

REFERENCES

Michell Wilson, "Female and Male Rates," *Suicide and Life Threatening Behavior*, Vol. 11, 3, Fall 81.

Marv Miller, "The Geography of Suicide." *Psychological Reports*, 1980.

"Teenage Suicide. The Final Cry." North Carolina Governor's Council on Children and Youth, May, 1985.

CHAPTER 3

The Theories: Why Would Anyone Choose to Die?

T he headlines read: "13-year-Old Kills Herself After Father Scolds Her for Smoking." Another newspaper reported the suicide of a 14-year-old boy because he had to wear braces. Are these reasons to want to die? How could a teenager who has a whole life ahead choose death as the solution to seemingly minor problems? Indeed, if we stop our efforts to understand the causes of suicide at such simplistic reasons, we do not do justice to the problem. The causes of suicide are many and varied. It is not like an illness for which researchers can isolate a germ in a test tube or develop a vaccine and thus halt the incidence of the disease. Instead of searching for a single cause, suicidologists take many approaches and investigate the problem of suicide by seeking information from several resources.

CRISIS THEORY

The Oriental definition of the word *crisis* is opportunity and danger. There is grave danger for the physical and emotional well-being of someone in crisis, and there is also hope that positive growth will occur as the crisis diminishes. Even though the experience of a crisis is subjective and individual, its course is somewhat predictable and its characteristics can be described.

We may think that a catastrophic event must happen to put someone into a crisis. A death of a loved one, flunking out of school, or an accident resulting in a severe handicap can be considered pretty horrendous. Could the breakup of a relationship between a 14-year-old girl and 15-year-old boy, or the death of a pet, cause someone to be in crisis? It is not the situation itself, but the emotional reaction to that situation that determines the crisis. That is an important distinction. Yes, the death of a pet or the breakup of a teenage relationship may be the precipitating event for a crisis. The situation or event itself cannot be judged as unimportant or the emotions dismissed as minor. What may be a slight setback for one person may be catastrophic for another. If someone reacts with intense emotions, he is in a crisis regardless of the importance of the situation to anyone else.

The emotions typically experienced in a crisis are intense anger, fright, or sadness. These emotions block a person's ability to use cognitive or reasoning abilities. It becomes extremely difficult to make decisions or to concentrate. It is not unusual for a person in crisis to declare how confused everything seems to be. Behavior may seem irrational as the person in crisis acts without the ability to foresee the consequences because of impaired judgment. Thinking becomes constricted. Instead of seeing many possibilities, the mind decides it is either/or, with no middle ground. "Either Jimmy makes up with me or I will never be happy again." "Either I kill myself or I will always feel this pain." It is like a horse wearing blinders, unable to see to left or right. Someone in a suicidal crisis may focus on suicide as the only alternative. It is the light at the end of the tunnel, because cessation of consciousness signifies the end of suffering.

Perhaps the most significant characteristic of someone in crisis is despair and hopelessness. The hopelessness says that it will never get better, and the thought of enduring the suffering forever is unbearable. Closely allied with hopelessness is helplessness. "There is nothing I or anyone can do to make it better." The person in crisis sees himself as having no control or power over what is happening. Furthermore, the sense of haplessness complicates the whole situation. Haplessness is unluckiness. No matter how diligent the effort, everything goes wrong. "Nothing will change, nothing will improve—so why try anymore?"

This line of thinking may be quite erroneous, but remember how intense emotions affect the reasoning. The perception of helplessness is all that counts. Everyone has the strength, the power to make choices and to solve problems, but when in crisis they temporarily lose touch with that power. The perception that they are out of control over what is happening puts them in a very weak and vulnerable position. The threat of suicide is one way of controlling or manipulating others. It may be maladaptive and tremendously dangerous, but it may work. Telling someone that you will kill yourself if he or she doesn't do as you wish is a sure way to stir things up—as well it should. The sense of powerlessness is an important part of crisis theory. It gives direction to crisis intervention counselors. A major objective is to help someone get in touch with that lost sense of power. Ways to do this are discussed in Chapter 6.

Another important aspect of crisis theory is the sense of isolation. No one cares, no one understands. How difficult it is to shoulder burdens alone! Despite having a family and plenty of friends, if the person in crisis thinks no one cares or understands he may as well be stranded on a desert island. This effect of a crisis can be devastating because the person may take drastic measures to communicate the need for attention and recognition of what is going on inside him. A suicide attempt then becomes that cry for help. It is a powerful cry, and the tears that fall burn into loved ones' hearts. A young suicide attempter wrote this poem.

Such is life

Such is life;
lonely and cold
traveling through
lost and old.
Such is life;
alone, no one there
Surviving, existing
love never to share.
Such is life;
no path to choose
Some of us are
born to lose.
Such is life
as it goes on.
Such is life,
a lonely song.
Such life I live.
Where do I
belong?

A crisis can be plotted on a chart to give a picture of the sequence of events. At the left of the chart is a horizontal line that represents homeostasis or equilibrium (stability). Most people function on a fairly even keel and can handle the stress that is inevitable in everyday life. If the stress increases, the crisis line becomes jagged with ups and downs, and the person is susceptible to responding to stressful events in a vulnerable manner. Then something happens that is the last straw. This precipitating event is the edge of the cliff, and the person takes a nose dive into a full-blown crisis.

The bottom of the line is the time when it is worst for the person in crisis. The pain is most intense. Anxiety is high and energy is low. This is *not* the time when suicide is most likely to occur. It takes energy to kill oneself, and in the depths of depression or in the peak of a crisis experience, one has insufficient energy to commit suicide. As the crisis seems to improve, the risk for suicide increases. If the decision to die is made while at the very bottom of the crisis chart, relief follows. Outward appearances show someone who is in the healing process. He may seek out friends, seem more relaxed, even smile and joke again. However, the relief comes from the hope and knowledge that the pain will soon be gone forever for he will be dead. Just the thought that such anguish and despair will not have to be borne anymore is sufficient to bring the relief. It is similar to dealing with stress that is generated when we face any large problem. We may wrestle mentally for days trying to decide which direction to take. Once the decision is made to try something, relief comes—even though the problem has not yet been solved. It is the decision that reduces the stress, not the solution. It is necessary to be very cautious with persons who seem to be coming out of

ANATOMY OF A CRISIS*

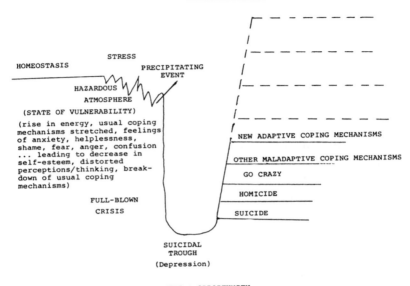

CRISIS = DANGER + OPPORTUNITY

_____

*Source: *Training Manual,* The Suicide and Crisis Center.

a crisis and have given warning signs of suicide. It may be important to help them protect themselves by removing weapons from easy access and making sure they are not alone at this time.

Of course, not all crises are resolved by suicide or a suicide attempt. The person may no longer be able to function and become immobilized, or may exhibit bizarre behavior and need hospitalization. The basic problem is temporarily put aside as the patient is cared for in a safe, secure environment. Another solution is homicide. If there is intense anger at another person, the crisis can be resolved by striking out and harming the person who is perceived as causing the crisis.

At this point in the crisis line, the person is taking action to fight off the emotional effects of the crisis. He may choose other maladaptive coping mechanisms. Stealing food, writing bad checks, making harassing telephone calls, or staying drunk or stoned may be ways of getting what is needed temporarily to ease the tension. These alternatives are maladaptive. The solution is only temporary and may even cause more problems. What is hoped is that new coping mechanisms will be learned. Tapping into old resources and seeking new ones may help someone work through the crisis to find appropriate and successful solutions. Notice what happens to the crisis line following the learning of new coping behavior. It continues upward and evens off at a level higher than the original level of functioning. The person has become stronger. The crisis experience has left him with new skills and a new inner power.

A crisis is time-limited. It cannot continue for more than six to eight weeks. Something has to give. The body cannot withstand that kind of stress for any longer period of time. If the crisis line follows the typical course, the person has a marvelous opportunity for growth. If the line is interrupted before that opportunity comes, there is extreme danger for the person's well-being.

A. THE MOTIVATIONS FOR SUICIDE

We come to understand from crisis theory that suicide accomplishes one main thing: It puts an end to the emotional pain that the person in crisis is suffering. The search for answers ultimately ends with the realization that people kill themselves to escape the pain and suffering in life that they are experiencing at that time. It is not death they seek, but an end to life as they know it. That is not really a contradictory statement. The key to understanding is the realization that suicide is only one of several possible escapes from living with the emotional pain and suffering. Tunnel vision prevents exploring other alternatives. Crisis intervention opens up new vistas and takes the blinders off the mind.

Suicide, or attempted suicide, serves different purposes for different people. One teen may plan that his final act in life will be one of defiance and revenge. Bill told the crisis counselor, "They will be sorry when I'm gone." His anger was seething inside, and he wanted to hurt his parents as he was hurting from their lack of acceptance of his behavior and respect for his growing sense of independence and freedom. What Bill was unable to think through was that, if he were dead, he would not be there to enjoy the revenge. His parents would mourn, but what would he accomplish for himself?

Vic, in Chapter 2, threatened to kill himself so often that Susan did not believe he would really do it. Vic had learned that a suicide threat was a powerful way of getting what he wanted. An actual attempt is even more effective in manipulating others. The fantasy of the frantic trip to the hospital, doctors working feverishly while the anxious family cries in the waiting room, may prompt self-destructive behavior with the hope of gaining attention and love that was withheld or not communicated.

Suicide is often described as a desperate cry for help. It actually is a form of communication, a way of telling others that things are not okay inside and that the person feels helpless to do anything about it. One young teen told the story of cutting her wrists one night. The bleeding stopped and she put bandages on them. No one said anything about the bandages the next day. Her mother may have noticed, but she didn't ask. Her girlfriends at school talked among themselves but thought it was none of their business. Everyone ignored her, and she was so hoping someone would pay attention to her so she could have someone with whom to share her feelings. She had purposely chosen a method that would not cause her to die. The suicide attempt was her hope that someone would notice and help her.

By far the majority of suicidal people do not want to die, but rather hope to accomplish something else with the suicide gesture or attempt. Revenge, manipulation, or seeking help are three motivating factors. Sometimes these motives are not present but there is a real desire to end the pain at all costs. There may be regret that the death will hurt others, but the pain is so intense that the regret is put aside. If life is this bad, death has to be better.[1]

B. SOCIOLOGICAL FACTORS

The suicide rate for adolescents has increased tremendously in the last three decades. In the search for reasons for this increase, attention must turn to the variables in our society, or factors that are different now from three decades ago. What are the sociological influences on teenage suicides?

Research reveals that there is a high positive correlation between the divorce rate and suicide among teenagers. As the divorce rate increases, so does the suicide rate. The breakup of the traditional family (mother, father, and children) by separation, divorce, or death is related to suicidal behavior in the children. In addition, adolescent suicides are more frequent in one-parent families. When

[1] Francine Klagsbrun. *Too Young to Die: Youth and Suicide.* Houghton Mifflin, 1976.

the family structure is not intact, the children are more vulnerable to a sense of isolation and guilt for having caused the family to fall apart. This is true even though the guilt may be irrational. Both parents are not available on a routine daily basis to support the child, serve as role models, and provide parental control. The resulting instability leaves the children more susceptible to the stress and pressures that are inevitable with adolescence. Grief over loss of family closeness, unity, and intimacy is a devastating effect of the splitting up of a family.

Émile Durkheim,[2] who was cited in Chapter 2, described the relationship between suicide and society. His theories still make sense today. The social institutions of our society are changing very quickly, sometimes leaving a void, sometimes leaving confusion. The family structure is not stable. Sexual freedom offers more choices to young people. Women are pursuing careers that used to be reserved for men, and the threat of nuclear war creates a hopeless attitude toward the future. The rapidity of this change creates unrest and anxiety and confusion in young people. Adolescence is a stage of development in which the maturing person searches for identity and his role in life. Durkheim predicted that suicide would be more common in societies such as ours that have a sudden change in social traditions, as it would be more likely for persons who have a sudden change in their individual role. For example, the loss of a job for a middle-aged man may mean loss of social status and a shattering of his life goals as well as the loss of his ability to provide for his family. He no longer knows his position in life, as a teenager is still struggling to find his.

Families are highly mobile in today's fast-paced, success-oriented society. A promotion may mean a transfer to

---

[2] Émile Durkheim. *Suicide, a Study in Sociology.* Free Press, 1951.

another part of the country; a loss of employment may take the family to another city where jobs are more plentiful. A move brings a change of schools for the kids and means leaving behind the friends and support groups that come from months or years of knowing one another and being together. Entering a new high school can be particularly tough. The cliques are already formed, the social structure is in place. It takes tremedous effort, know-how, and luck to break in and be accepted. To gain a leadership position may be an even more difficult struggle. The secur ity associated with a well-defined role may have been lost when the family moved. When things get difficult, who is there to turn to if your best friend is a thousand miles away? Again there is a sense of loss, and again the teen is more open to choosing suicide as a solution to an unacceptable situation.

There are other shifting patterns of family life that may have an influence on the teenage suicide rate. More and more women are choosing to enter the work force instead of accepting the traditional role of full-time mom and housewife. The children are left with child-care agencies or shuttled from relative to relative. All too often they come home from school to an empty house. When the family is together in the evening the parents are tired and still have the household chores to do. Quality time for family interaction is sparse. The family pattern is markedly different from a few generations ago when grandparents, aunts and uncles, and cousins all lived under one roof. That extended family created a crowded home, but someone was always available, someone was there to listen and interact with the children.

Sociologists who study the phenomenon of the increase in the suicide rate among adolescents suggest that the competition for recognition and opportunity is stiffer now because the population of teens is larger. More kids are competing for positions on the football team or the cheer-leading squad, acceptance to a prestigious college, or the part-time job. With changing patterns in population, it is predicted that the number of people in the 15–24 age bracket will decline. With that change, the teenage suicide rate may also decline.

C. DEPRESSION AND MENTAL ILLNESS

The most common reason people give for wanting to die is unhappiness. When a deep melancholia envelops a person he feels no hope, no joy, and the reasons for living can be far overshadowed by the desire to die. Not everyone who becomes depressed also becomes suicidal, nor is everyone who is suicidal also depressed. However, the majority of young people who commit suicide exhibit some symptoms of severe depression.

It is quite normal to react to disappointment and failure with sadness and maybe an inner anger. When a young girl is rejected after her first job interview, she may have a sense of inadequacy and be embarrassed to tell her friends that she didn't get the job. The athlete who trained hours each day for months loses the big race. He is ashamed and dejected that because of his failure the team did not bring the trophy back to their school. The student who makes straight A's does not earn the recognition of Merit Scholar and feels bewildered and hurt. Temporary depression may cause these young people to become moody and irritable for a few hours, a few days, or even a few weeks. It may be difficult for them to pay attention in class or smile when meeting a friend in the hall, but situational depression is a normal expression of disappointment and disappears with the passage of time and other distractions.

Most people have low self-regard when experiencing failure. Other situations that have to be faced from time to time cause acute feelings of grief and loss. When a close friend or family member dies, the mourning includes shock, numbness, tears, and yearning. Those same feelings may surface when a close relationship breaks up, especially when it is someone else who forces the breakup. The grief reaction is the same, and it may take a while to progress through the healing process.

On the other hand, clinical depression is a deep, despairing experience. It may leave a person struggling with a decision between living and dying. A feeling of worthlessness and low self-esteem is at the core of deep depressive states. The causes of clinical depression are not always understood. Becoming depressed after a failure or loss is normal but temporary. If the depression continues or if no particular situation triggers the despair, it is called clinical depression. It may have several causes. Sometimes it is due to a chemical imbalance in the body and can be treated with antidepressant drugs and psychotherapy.

It has been recognized only within the last few decades that children also suffer from depression. We used to view childhood as a carefree stage of development. Now it is understood that both children and adolescents do display their own signs of depression. Childhood suicide is rare, but it does occur. An eight-year-old boy committed suicide in Texas following the divorce of his parents. An eleven-year-old girl in California killed herself after her father punished her for smoking. Research studies are beginning to reveal that even preschool children express self-destructive tendencies. A nine-year-old boy once contacted a crisis center by phone to ask for help for his five-year-old brother. The younger sibling had once set fire to his own room and periodically held a toy pistol to his head to act out his own death. He was morose and unruly. Their mother seemed to be at a loss as to what to do. Discipline and spanking seemed to have no effect in controlling his behavior. When she came to realize the seriousness of his behavior, she sought counseling for herself and her family.

Symptoms of depression may be camouflaged in children and thus not recognized by adults. Young children may not express their sadness as adults do. They may act out their feelings through the constant motion of hyperactivity and impulsivity with little care for caution. A depressed child may become irritable, talk about physical complaints, have trouble sleeping, and turn into a "picky" eater. His parents may describe him as a difficult child.

Adolescent depresson begins to resemble the depressive states seen in adulthood as well as continue some symptoms seen in the earlier years. One of the outstanding characteristic is shifts in mood. One day the depressed teen may seen normal and happy and the next day be down in the dumps and have the blues. He may seem irritable and agitated, with self-reproach and feelings of worthlessness. It is difficult for the young person experiencing depression to concentrate and maintain interest or pleasure in activities. He may act bored. A change in sleeping and eating habits, a downward swing in school performance, drug and alcohol abuse, truancy and delinquency, or sexual promiscuity can signify depression.

Schizophrenia is a severe mental disorder that increases the risk of suicide in young people. Certainly not all suicidal teens are mentally ill, but if psychosis is present, the episodes of hallucination may trigger a suicide attempt. The psychosis causes the person to be unable to distinguish between what is real and what is not real. He progressively withdraws into himself, paying attention to his inner self and the voices no one else hears. His outward behavior reflects this inner world and makes no sense to anyone else. It is possible for a schizophrenic to become violent and harm himself and others. One of the considerations for commitment to a mental institution is the possibility of self-injury. Hospitalization does not guarantee safety, but it offers some degree of protection in a possibly explosive situation.

Another disease that may lead to suicidal thoughts and attempts is manic-depressive psychosis. The person shifts from periods of elation and wild jubilation to the depths of despair. During the manic phase he feels euphoric and full of energy. Manic people may also become unreasonably angry and violent. During the depressive phase the energy and good cheer disappear. The mood shifts to profound sadness, and suicide becomes a real danger as the person sees little reason for continuing life.

D. REBELLION AND ESCAPE

Substance abuse is often cited as a cause of suicide among young people. The nagging uneasiness of not fitting into a comfortable role within a loving, close family, or the stress that is felt from the pressure to achieve and succeed in "acceptable" endeavors may lead teens to escape into the euphoria and oblivion of the drug world. Drugs temporarily deaden the fears and anxieties that come with the stress an adolescent faces as he prepares himself for the adult world. Mood-changing drugs appeal to adolescents in a stressful period of rapid psychological and physical change. Alcohol and drugs are readily available, and teens are faced with choices at a time when they are preoccupied with acceptance by their peers and may not be adequately prepared to make a decision to use or not to use drugs. Drugs and alcohol may be an escape from problems but then become a problem in themselves. Heavy usage prevents normal functioning and increases the likelihood of failure and rejection. That alienation and failure feed into feelings of isolation and worthlessness, which are two of the dynamics of suicidal tendencies.

Rebellion by a teenager against an unacceptable world and a perceived nonproductive phase of life may take other forms. The pent-up anger, frustration, and depression may unleash antisocial behavior. The runaway, delinquent, or sexually promiscuous adolescent creates a life that has few bonds with the community and few dreams for the future.

Janice chose to attempt suicide rather than tell her mother she was pregnant. "Mother would kill me if she knew," was her reply when asked why she didn't let her mother know. She failed to see the inconsistency in her statement. If she had died from her attempt, the family would have learned of her pregnancy anyway. Embarrassment, shame, confusion, and fear led her to seek a dramatic way to communicate her turmoil.

E. LOW SELF-ESTEEM: FAMILY RELATIONSHIPS AND LACK OF COMMUNICATION

Underlying the decision to die is a feeling of unworthiness. "I don't deserve to live. I am not a worthwhile person." The decision to commit suicide is begun in early childhood. If a child gets the message, "Don't be who you are" or "Don't exist" from the parents, and that message is repeated often enough, the child may come to the conclusion that life is not worthwile. When life gets tough with the stresses of adolescence and the teenager loses control, the outcome may be suicide. Others, when they get into a crisis, do not commit suicide because they decided early in childhood that their life had value.

Self-esteem is the evaluation of the self by standards that the person sets for himself. Who would he like to be? If there is a distance between that ideal and who he thinks he really is, a conflict arises and there is internal dissatisfaction and a personal lack of acceptance. A child can gain self-esteem and feel good about himself if he is loved unconditionally by others. He is validated and approved of, not because of what he does, but simply for himself. He also gains feelings of satisfaction that come from success experiences. He derives pleasure from a newly learned skill or accomplishment and receives attention and praise as well.

These attitudes are learned within the family structure. It is most difficult for a child to love himself if he thinks that he is unloved by others. He may strive to meet his parents' goals for him because he thinks he has to earn their love along with their respect. If those goals are unrealistic or unattainable, the child is burdened with frustration and hostility builds up. He blames himself for not deserving his parents' love. In some homes children are mistreated and abused, and it is obvious how they can come to feel unloved and unwanted. But other families communicate the same message in a more insidious yet equally harmful way. The abuse need not be physical. It can be just as devastating if the atmosphere is cold and rejecting. Parents are encouraged to express their love for their children by touching and hugging them and telling them of it. It should not just be assumed. A child needs to feel it and hear it over and over.

When a child feels this unconditional love and acceptance, he is more likely to be open and direct in communicating with his parents. No matter what he does, he will still be loved. If he fears rejection and punishment or lack of understanding, he will learn to avoid confiding in them. If the teenager does not see his parents as a resource, he may view the world as a pretty confusing place when he finds himself in a crisis situation.

This note was left for her parents by a girl who committed suicide at the age of 14.

Let me go, set me free
away from everything they want me to be

I'm a human and I make mistakes.
I don't want to be like them, not fakes.
If I can't be or find what I can do
I'll have to forget about life and yes, even you.

Maybe I shouldn't be here at all.
Someday I'll break and can't ever come back.
There's something inside of me that's
pulling further and further off the track.

I'm sorry, I'm sorry, won't you
ever forgive?

Goodbye, goodbye. There's no reason to live.

F. SUFFERING A LOSS

The only person Stan knew who died was his grandmother. He was seven years old at the time. His parents decided it would be best that he not be exposed to the funeral and burial experience, so he was left with neighbors for a couple of days as the traditional grieving ritual was planned and carried out. His parents wanted to spare him the hurt and sadness. They thought he was too young to understand, so he was not allowed to participate in the family's grief. He was bewildered when he was told that his grandmother was on a long, long trip and would be happy now because she was in heaven. He had always been close to her, and he missed her terribly. He had no outlet to express his sadness and yearning. His parents did not cry in front of him nor talk about his grandmother's death.

Stan was not permitted to develop a coping method that would help him face a loss. The grief he experienced when his grandmother died was similar to the feeling he had the next year when his dog disappeared from the yard one day and never returned. His father told him he was a big boy and should not cry when he couldn't find the dog. Those feelings recurred when he had his first serious girlfriend at sixteen and the family moved to another state. He planned to call, to write, to go back and visit as often as he could, but within a few weeks his girlfriend told him it just wouldn't work and she thought it best that they both date other kids. Stan was in a crisis. He had no built-in mechanism to help him handle his feelings. The opportunities had been there, but he had not learned how to cope with loss.

The common thread in teenage suicide is the reaction to a loss. Something happens, there is a precipitating event, and the response is grief. It is very similar to what a grieving person goes through after the death of a loved one. The most difficult of losses is the loss of a love relationship. It could be through death as in Stan's case when he was seven. It could be the breakup of a boy-girl relationship as when he was sixteen. The loss may come when a friend moves away or parents separate.

Other kinds of loss also trigger grief. When failure is experienced, the loss of self-esteem may bring those same feelings. Additional shame and anger may compound the grief when a prized goal is not attained. If illness or injury robs a youth of vitality and health, he may mourn that loss, view the future as bleak, and feel helpless to change it. Not all teens who are handicapped respond to loss in this way. Some tackle the adversity head-on with vigor and create a satisfying, pleasurable life in spite of the handicap.

G. SUICIDE EPIDEMICS

One of the most baffling phenomena in recent years has been the clustering of suicides among young people who live in the same community or attend the same school. Plano and Clearlake, Texas, Westchester County, New York, Bergenfield, New Jersey, and Chicago, Illinois, all have experienced a series of teenage suicides in a short period of time. Many questions are raised regarding the influence that one suicide has on another adolescent who may be depressed or seeking a solution to unendurable psychological pain. Is suicide contagious? Can one death cause someone else to be suicidal?

In these epidemics, each teenager who committed suicide knew of the previous suicides by personal acquaintance, by word of mouth, or through media coverage. Behavior is known to be copied or imitated if a person identifies with another. Much of our behavior is learned in that manner. A small child learns to adopt feminine or masculine ways by identifying with the mother or father. Advertising takes advantage of this principle. A striking example was a public service television spot: A young father picks up a twig and tosses it; the little boy then tosses a twig. The man kicks a stone, and the little boy kicks a stone in the same manner. Then they sit down under a tree and the father takes a cigarette out of a pack and lights it. The little boy picks up the pack and looks at it. The message is clear.

We model after heroes in books or after movie stars. Whenever a famous person such as Freddie Prince or Marilyn Monroe commits suicide, it is common for a rash of suicides to follow. The stronger the identification, the more likely the imitation. The closer the relationship, such as parent and child or sibling and sibling, the stronger the identification. In Mesquite, Texas, a father committed suicide. Exactly one year later his 12-year-old son committed suicide with the same gun sitting in the same kitchen chair. The father's suicide left a message for his son that it is okay to kill yourself if the emotional pain you are suffering is intolerable. When a family member commits suicide, the risk is higher for another family member to die by suicide.

Friends also model after friends. Note the teenage fads in styles of dress and popular music. It is not likely that the suicide of a friend will cause another to become suicidal. However, if another teenager is already suffering or in a crisis, it is reasonable to believe that he may choose to imitate or model the solution of suicide to end the psychological pain and permanently eliminate the unbearable stress. Concern for the friends of a teenage suicide victim is well deserved, and attention needs to be given to their grief and emotional state.

There is some fear that the media play a role in the clusters of teenage suicide. If the reporting sensationalizes or glamorizes the death, suicide may become more attractive to another teenager who is seeking attention. The act of suicide may become romantic as in the story of *Romeo and Juliet*, and thus seem a way to become immortalized through headlines and features stories. The permanence of death is lost sight of in the fantasy. However, if the reporting of teenage suicide is treated as news and includes some educational information, as is usually the case, it can be considered beneficial. The media can become a means to teach about warning signs and community resources. Most suicidologists agree that one of the objectives in suicide prevention is to teach the clues to suicide.

There is little agreement among researchers and professional suicidologists regarding the relationship between televised films and the numbers of suicides and attempted suicides by teenagers. Two studies published in 1986 indicated a possible link between the showing of fictional and real news stories about teenage suicides and a higher than expected number of young people attempting and completing suicide. After these studies were published, several other people repeated the research to see how reliable the data were. At this time it is premature to conclude that television films about suicide have a fatal effect. If young people watch them, however, it is advisable to watch them with parents to share the feelings and thoughts that are aroused.

More research is needed before we thoroughly understand clusters of suicide and the contagion theory as well as the effects of the media on the epidemies of suicide that have occurred in some communities in the United States.

H. SUMMARY

As we try to understand why young people kill themselves, it becomes clear that we are dealing with a very complicated matter. Any cause alone would be too simple an explanation. Put together, we see a bleak picture of teens who are under more psychological stress than ever before.

Author David Elkind[3] recognizes this as he discusses the new freedoms young people have in today's society "to abuse drugs and to flout adult authority. At the same time, they are less prepared than ever before to manage these new freedoms." They lack ability to respond to fast-changing social traditions. For some, the stress becomes unbearable.

A crisis occurs when someone reacts to a situation with intense emotions and is unable to use cognitive abilities to solve the problem. He feels hopeless, helpless, and hapless. He has a sense of isolation; no one cares or understands. A crisis may trigger a suicide attempt because the person in crisis is unable to think of other options. The most dangerous time for suicide is during the beginning of apparent improvement. A crisis lasts no more than six to eight weeks. If a person works through the crisis, there is opportunity for growth as he learns new coping strategies.

The decision to kill oneself comes after a precipitating event during a crisis. It may have been incubating for a long time, but the decision itself is strongly affected by an immediate situation. If mental illness is present, the risk of suicide increases and hospitalization is sometimes necessary to protect the teenager from harming himself.

The two factors that are important in helping the developing child decide to choose life, even when the going gets tough, are having self-esteem and experiencing loss. How one judges himself determines his perceived worth. If he is loved unconditionally he has a better chance of

3 David Elkind. *All Grown Up and No Place to Go. Teenagers in Crisis*. Addison-Wesley, 1984.

not having a gap between who he thinks he is and who he would like to be. Experiencing losses during childhood helps to build up a repertoire of coping skills that may be used in a crisis. Loss of a relationship is the most common precipitating event for a teenage suicide attempt.

The phenomenon of suicide clusters among teenagers is baffling. How one suicide influences another teen to commit suicide is not known exactly. It is theorized that one death does not cause the problem that leads to another attempt, but rather it models a solution to an already existing problem.

I. DISCUSSION QUESTIONS

1. What are some common stresses that teenagers face today?
2. Describe what happens to someone who is in a crisis situation.
3. Why is it so difficult to list the causes of teenage suicide?
4. Why are there more teenage suicides now than there were three decades ago?
5. What changes in our social traditions have you observed in your lifetime? Compare your life-style to that of your parents when they were your age.
6. What measures are taken in your school to help new students become adjusted?
7. How can a parent help a child develop a strong sense of self-esteem?
8. Describe losses you have experienced in your lifetime and how you learned to handle them.
9. How do you think the news reports have influenced the epidemics of teenage suicide?

REFERENCES

Training Manual. Suicide and Crisis Center, Dallas, Texas, 1985.

CHAPTER 4

Warning Signs: How Can You Tell When Someone Is Suicidal?

Brad Davis' parents sat on the sofa of the comfortable meeting room in The Crisis Center. They moved closer to each other, and Mr. Davis held Mrs. Davis' hand as she began to tell the other members of the support group about Brad's suicide. "He wasn't like those other teenagers we read about in the newspapers. He was a happy boy and was doing so well in school. I will never understand why he wanted to die. We had no way of knowing anything was wrong. Sure, he was acting a little different lately, but all teenagers are so moody. We just thought he was going through a spell. If only we had known..."

As Mr. and Mrs. Davis described the weeks leading up to Brad's death, it became apparent that actually Brad had attempted over and over to let those around him know that he was thinking about suicide. On the day of his suicide he told a friend at school that he was planning to kill himself. She didn't tell anyone because she had promised to keep it a secret. Anyway, she thought Brad was being dramatic and didn't believe he would ever go through with it. Mr. Davis had noticed that a gun was missing from the cabinet a week ago, and when Brad drove out of the driveway that last evening he watched his son go and wondered whether he should have mentioned it. Mrs. Davis thought Brad was losing weight. He had always had a good appetite. After all, he was a growing teenager. It seemed as though she was buying a new pair of jeans every other week to keep up with the rapid growth of his long, lanky legs. She did think he wasn't eating or sleeping well lately, but she attributed that to the early fall heat.

These survivors were dealing with a tremendous amount of guilt in addition to their grief. "If only . . ., if only we had known." Ambivalence leads suicidal people to communicate their pain and need of attention. Very few people who attempt suicide are not ambivalent. Few do not let others know in one way or another that they are thinking of killing themselves. Over 80 percent exhibit the classic warning signs.[1]

Professional suicidologists are convinced that suicides can be prevented because so many suicidal people try to let others know. If people who come in contact with someone who is in crisis could recognize those signals, they would be in a better position to give support and get help.

Read the following clues carefully and keep them in mind if you think a friend may be in a crisis.

[1] Patricia Davis. *Suicidal Adolescents*. Charles C. Thomas, 1983.

A. VERBAL CLUES

Brad had told a school friend that he wanted to die. He was direct and clear about his intent. The friend chose not to believe him. When Sandy's husband, Vic, threatened suicide, he also was direct, even putting a gun to his head. Sandy, too, did not believe Vic would ever carry out his threat. Brad expressed his suicidal intentions only once, on the day he died. Vic repeated his threats over a period of several years. Neither young man was taken seriously, and neither survived.

Statements such as, "I am going to commit suicide," or "I don't want to live anymore," are fairly clear-cut messages. It may be hard to imagine how anyone could not understand them, but it must be realized that people are likely to react to the word suicide with fear and confusion. They don't want to believe what they are hearing so they don't believe it, and the message goes unheeded.

There are other, more subtle ways people tell those around them that they are thinking about suicide:

"Soon I won't be hurting so much anymore."
"I wish I could go to sleep and never wake up."
"They will be sorry when I'm gone."
"I wish I had never been born."
"You won't have to put up with me much longer."
"I wonder what it is like to be buried in a grave."
"I don't think I will be able to manage much longer."
"Do you think dying hurts?"
"They would be better off without me."

Such an indirect statement communicates the desire to die. You have to stop and think why the person is saying it. The hope is that you will understand and be willing to ask and talk about the meaning behind the statement.

Students may express a preoccupation with death and dying through written assignments and poetry or even artwork. Teachers and classmates are in an excellent position to pick up on these warning signs if they are able to recognize them.

B. BEHAVIORAL CHANGES

Depression is the main clinical symptom of suicidal people. As we saw in Chapter 3, depression may manifest itself differently in teenagers than in adults. It is easier to recognize than childhood depression, but it may take on added dimensions of impulsiveness, impatience, or restlessness. This uneasiness pushes a depressed young person to take action to relieve the tension. He or she may act out, become unruly and wild, get into trouble at school or with the law, and be described as "unmanageable" at home. On the other hand, a moody teen such as Brad Davis may act bored and uninterested and mope around the house.

Depression manifests itself in many ways in teenagers. One would expect sadness, with few smiles and frequent tears. Depressed persons may tire easily, partly because they aren't sleeping well, and partly for lack of energy. Changes in sleeping patterns and changes in eating habits with either weight gain or weight loss are major clues that depression may be present. Sometimes it is accompanied by physical complaints, real or imagined. The uneasiness may be expressed as discouragement about the future and as sharp self-criticism, self-depreciation, and guilt. The teenager may be displeased with his physical appearance and talk of not liking the way he looks. It is common for a suicidal teen to become unkempt and ignore personal hygiene. Withdrawal from social contacts or activities is also typical.

Not all of these symptoms need be present for someone to be depressed. The presence of only one or two may indicate something else, such as a physical problem, or perhaps be part of the normal reaction to the relatively sudden physical, sexual, and emotional changes of adolescence. Depression affects different people in different ways. The danger is that it can generate a self-loathing and feeling of worthlessness that may very well motivate the depressed person to eradicate the hated target—himself.

With all of this going on, a student's schoolwork is bound to be affected. It may be very difficult to complete assignments, concentrate in class, or maintain good grades. When the achievement level lowers, the feeling of worthlessness and the low self-esteem may intensify, feeding right into the depression that was present in the first place.

Another symptom of depression is withdrawal. Interest in being with other people slackens off. When he is feeling low he doesn't have the enjoyment that comes with the frivolity or hoopla of a gang of friends having a good time. When he is at home he may retreat to his room to read, or lose himself in music, or simply do nothing.

Shirley had always shown an interest in a career in medicine. It would follow a long tradition of doctors, dentists, and nurses in the family. After graduation from high school she was accepted to a large state university to work toward her RN degree. She looked forward to the social life as well as the academic challenge. The first couple of days on campus went well. She liked her roommate and enjoyed the orientation events and settling into the life of the dorm. She was excited about the beginning of classes and wanted to succeed in college so that her family would be proud of her. At the same time she was afraid that she wouldn't be able to do the academic work. College classes were supposed to be a lot harder than high school.

She spent most of her time studying and had little energy
left for anything else. Her roommate joined a sorority and
spent little time with her. Shirley didn't put any effort
into making new friends. She missed her family and found
herself becoming more and more depressed. At midterm
she dropped out of school and went home.

Her mother urged her to continue her studies at the
junior college and then reenter the university the following
year, but Shirley didn't want to talk about it. She no longer
wanted to take nursing courses, and in fact nothing seemed
interesting to her. She spent her time sitting around the
house during the day and watching TV at night because
she couldn't sleep. Her parents had trouble accepting her
unproductive behavior and were confused by the changes
they observed in her. The days stretched into weeks and
Shirley became more and more withdrawn. She didn't help
with the housework or go out much. Her mother recognized
her unhappiness and hoped that it would pass with time,
but it didn't. A family friend recommended that the parents tell Shirley that enough was enough and they would
not put up with her laziness anymore. As difficult as it was
for her, Shirley's mother decided Shirley needed to get a
job. The longer she moped around, the worse it seemed to
get. She gave Shirley an ultimatum: Either go back to
school or get a job and support herself. They argued and
Shirley rushed out of the house, taking her mother's purse
and car keys with her.

The police came to the house four hours later to tell the
parents that Shirley was in the hospital following a suicide
attempt. She had driven to the city park and rolled the car
down a boat ramp into the water. A passerby observed the
partially submerged car and called the police. Shirley was
pulled from the water unconscious but alive. She had a
second chance at life.

The important thing about behavioral clues is to be aware of a change in how someone acts. If the person is depressed, the change in eating or sleeping patterns may be most obvious. A change in grades or a change in interest in other people or activities may indicate a serious problem.

When an older person has made up his mind to attempt suicide, he may do things to prepare for his own death. He may write a will or check an existing one to make sure everything is in order. He makes plans to care for the family and to tie up loose business ends. A young person makes a will in essence by giving away prized possessions. He wants those things that meant something to him to be given to someone he cares for. A camera, tape collection, clothes, or even a cherished car might be given to a best friend. If a ninety-five-year-old great grandmother goes around her house and designates each piece of furniture or hand-painted china cup for a grandniece or great grandchild, it does not mean she is suicidal. At that age she has accepted death as imminent and is letting go of the material things in her life. If a thirty-five-year-old or an adolescent does the same thing, it is time to be concerned, for it may mean that they too are preparing for death.

Someone who is suicidal may no longer protect him or herself, having stopped caring what happens. Consequently someone who isn't sure about life or death may take risks and have frequent accidents. Driving eighty miles an hour on a busy freeway or walking the dog in the park at two in the morning may indicate a "so what" or "who cares" attitude. Self-destructive tendencies may emerge in an obsessive interest in dangerous sports such as sky diving, race car driving, or bull riding. Certainly not every race car driver is suicidal, but it could be a clue and needs to be considered along with other behavioral and verbal warning signs.

It should be of special concern if any of these clues are present and there has been a prior suicide attempt. Once someone has used such an attempt to communicate the emotional pain that is being experienced, he is more likely to do so again. It is not true that he would have gotten the frustrations, the fear, the desperateness out of his system by the first attempt. It is a way of communicating, of asking for help. "Someone pay attention to me, hear my cry, understand how much I hurt." If he has not learned other ways to solve problems or get what he wants, he is at greater risk of attempting suicide again when another crisis occurs. Eighty percent of those who die by suicide have attempted it before.

C. SITUATIONAL WARNING SIGNS

When events occur that cause severe stress, some people react with confusion and intense emotion. Others are able to tap their internal strengths, use available resources, and manage to cope without getting into crisis. It is worthwhile to review the situations that commonly lead to crisis and a suicide attempt in young people.

The most dangerous experience is suffering a loss of relationship. The loss may be through death or separation or, as in the case of a double suicide in Plano, Texas, when the parents of two young lovers insisted they break up, the threat of a loss. The grief response of overwhelming yearning is similar. If the young person is floundering and has not learned how to take care of himself after losing someone or something precious to him, he may think that the grief will last forever and that despair becomes intolerable.

When a teenager who has difficulty communicating with his parents experiences a crisis, he may not have the family available for support. He may develop a deep sense of isolation and think he is going it alone. Statements like, "I could never tell them, they just don't listen," or "All he does is tell me it is my fault. I'm tired of being called stupid or lazy," indicate a rift in the communication link and should be a red flag of warning.

Other situations that suicidal teens experience are drug and alcohol abuse, pregnancy, delinquency, and trouble at school. Acting out in ways that are unacceptable to society is related to the incidence of suicide. Teens who are placed in juvenile detention centers or young unwed mothers who seek abortion are most likely to threaten or attempt suicide. The presence of mental or serious physical illness are situations that should be taken into consideration, particularly if there are also behavioral and verbal warning signs.

D. SUMMARY

Eighty percent of those who attempt or complete suicide give warning signs that indicate ambivalence and are a cry for help. For the sake of clarification, these clues may be divided into three categories: verbal, behavioral, and situational.

> Verbal: Direct statements about suicide.
> Indirect or subtle statements indicating a wish to die.
> Behavioral: Sadness and crying.
> Withdrawal from social contacts and activities.
> Disinterest in previous activities, hobbies, sports, or school.

Inability to complete assignments, drop
in grades.
Confusion, mood shifts, impatience or
impulsivity.
Inability to concentrate, boredom and
listlessness.
Change in sleep patterns.
Change in eating habits.
Giving away of prized possessions.
Prior suicide attempts.
Obsession with death.
Increased use of drugs or alcohol.
Lack of energy.
Guilt, self-reproach.
Sense of worthlessness and low self-
esteem.
Feelings of hopelessness.

Situational: Loss of significant relationship.
Recent move(s).
Family   disruption   (unemployment,
separation).
Trouble with the law.
Unwanted pregnancy.
Poor communication/relationship with
parents.
Problems with school or employment.
Serious physical illness.
Mental illness.

E. DISCUSSION QUESTIONS

1. Why would someone act differently if he were suicidal?
2. Describe what it is like to be depressed. What can you
   do to overcome those sad feelings?

3. Which of the warning signs do you think are most significant?
4. If you have known anyone to attempt suicide, did he exhibit any clues to his intention? What did he do or say to let others know he was thinking of dying?
5. Why is teaching the warning signs an important part of suicide prevention programs?

REFERENCES

Edwin S. Shneidman and Norman L. Farberow, eds. *Clues to Suicide*. McGraw-Hill, 1957.

PART III

CRISIS INTER- VENTION COMMUNI- CATION SKILLS

CHAPTER ◇ 5

All About Feelings:

Listening and Talking

"**N**o one understands!" Jane confided to the crisis counselor at the other end of the phone. It was 11:30 at night and Jane was sitting on the edge of her bed with a bottle of her mother's sleeping pills in her hand. "It seems as though there is a barrier between you and your parents and you feel so alone with the hurt and pain. That makes it even more difficult to bear," replied the counselor. "If only they would listen," said Jane. "All they do is tell me what to do and that I'll get over it. I don't think they know what it is like to have this happen. What's worse, I don't think they care! I'm not ever going to get over it and I can't face another day at school!" The counselor paused and then said, "You sound frustrated and desperate because you think that your parents are not giving you the support you need or even caring about you or what you want, or trying to understand."

This is a typical conversation between a teenager in crisis and a counselor answering the phone at a suicide prevention center. The counselor realized that Jane was experiencing intense feelings of shame, anger, and fear and was needing so much to share those strong emotions. Jane was trying to decide if life was worth living. The turmoil within her made it very difficult for her to explore other solutions to her problems. The counselor's role was to listen to those feelings and help Jane know that she was understood. Even if Jane did not directly express what she was feeling, the counselor would listen to the music behind the words. That brings the dark, mysterious aspect of the emotion out into the light of day so it can be examined and dealt with more easily. So often a suicidal person laments that no one understands. What that statement means is that no one understands how they *feel*. They see themselves as isolated and alone. Even if loving parents, friends, and many others are present in the person's everyday life, when those feelings are not acknowledged, it seems like battling the whole world all alone.

A. IMPORTANCE OF COMMUNICATING FEELINGS

Communicating one's feelings is not the usual way of talking. It is even more rare for the listener to reflect those feelings back to the speaker to demonstrate that they are understood. This is not surprising, because communicating at a feeling level is simply not taught to children. Children are taught how to think, how to reason, how to behave, how to do things, how to stay out of trouble, and how to please adults. The feeling or emotional side of a child is usually ignored or squelched by parents, teachers, and others.

For example, Scott, age nine, comes home from school, slams the back door, and throws his books down on the kitchen table exclaiming, "I hate school." What are the responses he is most likely to hear?

1. You are not supposed to hate. Don't ever let me hear you say that!
2. What did you do now?
3. No you don't!
4. Don't slam the door.
5. Tomorrow will be a better day.
6. Hurry up and get ready for dinner.
7. Tell me what happened.

How many moms (or dads) would let Scott know that his feelings are important and that someone understands how he feels? In #1 it is pointed out that hate or even anger is a negative feeling. You are *not supposed* to get angry; there *should* be room in your heart for only love and joy. Number 2 would most likely put Scott on the defensive. "Oh, oh, Mom is blaming me again; now I have to tell her what I did and argue with her that it wasn't my fault." Number 3 denies the feeling at all. But regardless of what is said, the anger feeling is there. If Scott does not learn to put a label on it, he may become confused. What is he experiencing if it is not anger? To purge the feeling of anger from our emotional repertoire is nearly impossible. Being human means feeling the whole range of emotions— even anger. What one does with that anger is a different matter. Scott may translate the angry response into a message that he is bad, but there is no good or bad to feelings; they just exist.

Scott has given someone a beautiful opportunity to become close, even intimate, by his statement, "I hate school!" One of the surest ways to push someone aside is to change the subject: "Don't slam the door." No wonder kids often see parents as nagging or bossy. Slamming doors bothers others, and the implication is that it is the parents' responsibility to teach children proper behavior. Slamming doors is reserved for dramatic adults only. "Do as I say, not as I do." "Hurry up and get ready for dinner," is another way of saying to Scott that his feelings are not important. It would not be unusual for Scott to turn that impression into the thought that *he* is not important. The lack of respect shown to children when they are told that their experiences and feelings are trivial is another way of saying they are unimportant. "Tomorrow will be a better day," is an attempt to reassure him that everything is going to be okay: but it may not be for Scott, and he probably is not asking for reassurance anyway. His mother doesn't need to take away his anger, only to acknowledge it. What Scott wants is to be heard, to be understood. The last statement, "Tell me what happened," does keep the communication lines open. Mom is interested and gives Scott her attention, but she has not made an attempt to let him know she understands how he feels. How much better for her to simply say, "Something happened at school today and you are really angry about that."

In Chapter 3 we saw what happens to a person who is in a crisis. The stressful situation or event leading to the crisis disrupts the stability, the equilibrium, the homeostasis, and the reaction is intense emotions. That gives us a clue how to help someone in crisis. *Feelings* cause a crisis. Thus, the first step in learning crisis intervention is to become aware of feelings and how to identify them.

B. THE EFFECTS OF FEELINGS

Think of the last time you were angry. What happened inside of you? Perhaps your stomach was tight, your breathing became rapid and shallow, and you perspired heavily. It seemed as if your heart beat faster, your eyes "flashed," your face was tight, and your voice became loud and shaky. Maybe you didn't announce to anyone that you were mad, but it probably was noticeable anyway.

Now think back to a time when you were feeling very sad. Your heart felt heavy, your stomach was upset and food tasted terrible, tears came easily, and smiles were difficult. You had trouble sleeping or had no energy to do your daily routine. You hoped someone would notice—not necessarily to cheer you up but just share the sadness and acknowledge your feelings.

When you become frightened, many of the same changes happen. When your mind tells your body that there is danger, the body prepares to meet that danger. The adrenalin starts pumping through the bloodstream and you actually tap an extra supply of strength. You become stronger to meet the threat or to run away from it if you choose. However, often we are faced with a situation without really knowing of what to be afraid. This is called anxiety. Anxiety is fear without knowing its source. It is much more insidious and dangerous to our well-being. It uses up a tremendous amount of energy, leaving the body weak and tired and uneasy.

All three of these categories of emotion are often intensified when someone is suicidal. Depression or sadness is the predominant symptom, but the other feelings may also be present. The first task for anyone who wishes to be a source of help and support to a friend in crisis is to be aware of feelings within him or herself. Then learn to put labels on those feelings. Increase your feeling-word vocabulary and your understanding of feelings by studying the accompanying lists of feelings. There are four basic categories of feelings: happy, sad, angry, and scared.

Levels of Intensity for Four Major Categories of Feelings

	Happy	Sad	Angry	Scared
STRONG	Excited	Hopeless	Desperate	Fearful
	Elated	Sorrowful	Exasperated	Panicky
	Hilarious	Drained	Furious	Afraid
	Buoyant	Lonely	Seething	Alarmed
	Overjoyed	Miserable	Enraged	Petrified
	Delighted	Dejected	Disgusted	Terrified
	Great	Woeful	Bitter	Hopeless
	Joyous	Dismal	Mad	Horrified
	Ecstatic		Incensed	Appalled
	Exuberant		Irate	Distraught
	Exhilarated		Outraged	Overwhelmed
				Frantic
MILD	Lighthearted	Upset	Annoyed	Insecure
	Cheerful	Dreary	Frustrated	Uneasy
	Up	Distressed	Agitated	Worried
	Happy	Down	Peeved	Apprehensive
	Proud	Discouraged	Resentful	Anxious
	Amused	Helpless	Cross	Scared
	Eager	Gloomy	Bothered	Foolish
	Festive	Dark		Edgy
	Enthusiastic			Bewildered
	Sunny			
	Hopeful			
	Jolly			
WEAK	Glad	Sorry	Uptight	Timid
	Good	Lost	Dismayed	Unsure
	Satisfied	Bad	Put down	Nervous
	Calm	Hurt	Disappointed	Tight
	Content	Ashamed	Bugged	Tense
	Serene	Unhappy	Irritated	Shaky
	Comfortable	Flat	Discontented	Restless
	Peaceful	Moody	Bored	Suspicious
	Tranquil			Hesitant
	Pleased			Concerned
				Uncomfortable

Within each category is a multitude of levels of intensity. For instance, *miserable* is a fairly strong description of a sad feeling, whereas *discouraged* is a milder word and *sorry* describes a weak feeling of sadness.

C. SEPARATING THOUGHTS AND FEELINGS

Feelings are a natural part of being human. They are partly a mental and partly a physical sensation. The physical component occurs in the central part of the body, the gut, but can spread like a shiver to the tips of your toes or a flush to your face. Feelings usually can be described by one word. On the other hand, thinking occurs in the head, and it usually takes at least a phrase to describe a thought. Thoughts are our intellectual language and deal with opinions, facts, attitudes. Thinking is the cognitive, reasoning process.

One of the most difficult habits to overcome in crisis intervention is *describing a thought* when the intention is to *express a feeling*. Remember Jane's pathetic plea to the crisis counselor that no one understood her. The counselor concentrated on understanding how she felt. He was precise and avoided the pitfall of using a thought to describe a feeling. Instead of commenting that Jane must *feel* that her parents were not giving her support, the counselor correctly identified that statement as a *thought*. With that *thought*, Jane may very well have a strong *feeling*, and the counselor identified the feeling as being desperate. How often do we hear statements such as, "I feel that my whole world is falling apart." What is the emotion described in that sentence? Hopelessness, alarm, worry, being upset? The whole world falling apart is a thought, not a feeling. The feeling has yet to be identified, and it is the task of a listener, a helper, or a crisis counselor to say, "You must be feeling upset."

One way to ensure the separation of thoughts and feelings is to notice sentences that have the word *like* or *that* after the word *feel*. *Like* and *that* are your clues that it is a thought that is being described, not a feeling. "I feel like it is going to be a pretty day." "I feel that he is being unfair." These statements may be alluding to a feeling but do not express it. How does the speaker *feel* if she *thinks* he is being unfair? Perhaps angry, bitter, nervous, helpless. It is not communicating at a feeling level. To change the statement by eliminating the word *that* and inserting a feeling word would correctly convey the emotion, "I feel angry when I think he is being unfair," is more direct and less confusing.

Another problem arises when we are learning to separate thoughts and feelings. We may use what we think are feeling words, but we actually are describing or evaluating a behavior. Rejection is a behavior. "I feel rejected," describes someone else's behavior: Someone rejected me. I may very well feel something when that happens. I could feel sad or angry. A correct way to express it would be to say, "I feel sad when I am rejected." Words like *inadequate* are evaluative words. Ask yourself how you would *feel* if you thought you were inadequate.

Exercise I   Thinking and Feeling Statements

Now is the time for some practice. Read the statements below. Circle the numbers of the statements in which the speaker is verbally expressing the feeling that he or she is experiencing. A statement may describe how the speaker would feel in the future if something happened; choose only the sentences that express present feeling. Also be sure to eliminate all statements that have *that* or *like* after the word *feel*. This exercise will help you learn to communicate feelings and separate them from thoughts. After you have chosen the sentences that express feelings, see page 158 of the Appendix for the Key to Identifying Feelings, Exercise I. Some of the answers may surprise you. It may seem that many of the incorrect statements (not feeling statements) should be correct (feeling statements). Indeed, there may be a feeling behind the words because these topics are emotion-laden, but the feelings have not been expressed by the words. Now go back and reword the thought statements to make them into feeling statements. "I feel like shouting when I get out of class on Friday afternoon," indicates a feeling of elation, joy, relief. Take out "feel like shouting" (which is a behavior, not a feeling) and substitute, "am delighted." "I am delighted when I get out of class on Friday afternoon," is an appropriate, direct statement of feeling.

1. I feel like shouting when I get out of class on Friday afternoon.

2. I feel happy when I hear that beautiful song.

3. I feel that no one really understands my problems.

4. I feel pushed around.

5. I'm thinking about going to the dentist, and right now I feel scared about it.

6. I feel terrified whenever I am around snakes.

7. I feel rejected since I wasn't invited to the party.

8. I feel like I'm ten feet tall whenever someone tells me that I'm smart.

9. From the things my friends say, I think I am a kind person.

10. I feel dominated by that pushy person.

11. I feel frightened walking through this dark alley tonight.

12. I feel really angry because I trusted my friend and she went and told when I asked her not to.

13. I feel like I haven't got a friend in the whole world.

14. I just crashed my car and I feel that it wasn't fair. After all, I just got it paid for last month!

15. I feel like you really care about me and my trouble.

16. I'm not really angry with you for what you said. I know that you didn't mean it the way it sounded.

17. I feel like my life is really getting better.

18. I feel anxious about reading this statement in front of the rest of the group.

19. I feel happy about buying some new clothes on Saturday, and at the same time, I feel worried about my folks getting the bill.

20. I feel so misunderstood.

D. ACTIVE LISTENING

When someone is so desperate, in so much turmoil that he wishes to die to stop the pain, the immediate objective in crisis intervention is to communicate understanding or empathy. This understanding conveys caring and helps establish rapport and a trusting relationship. Once the feeling has been identified, the speaker needs to hear from the listener what has just been communicated. In other words, the listener proves to the speaker that the feeling expressed or implied has been understood. If the speaker has not used a feeling word, the listener must guess what that feeling might be. If the speaker expresses the desire to die, the feeling may very well be fear and terror because dying is scary. The crisis intervention technique of active listening is to identify, accept, and reflect the feeling.

There is danger in the temptation to change the feeling by refusing to acknowledge or accept what has been communicated. We don't want people to be sad, angry, or afraid because we are uncomfortable. "Don't feel that way," "There is nothing to be scared about," or "You don't really mean that": Those statements are put-downs and are disrespectful of the person expressing the feeling. Another pitfall is to question the feeling. "Why do you feel that way?" Feelings don't need to be justified. They just exist.

It may not always be apparent what feeling is being expressed because a feeling word has not been used. It may seem that an easy way to find out how someone feels is simply to ask, but by asking you have lost your magic power of understanding. You have indicated your interest and that is a plus, but you have gained nothing toward being empathetic. It is much more powerful to imagine how you would feel if you said those words and to reflect that understanding by saying "You feel—." Put in a feeling word to complete the sentence. Also do not tell the speaker that you understand. You may very well understand, but you do not convey that understanding unless you prove it by identifying, accepting, and reflecting the feeling. If you say you understand, then continue with, "You feel happy" (or sad, or angry, or scared).

Exercise II   Stimulus Statements I

Imagine what the speaker is feeling who makes the statements in this multiple-choice exercise. Identify the feeling and practice active listening by choosing the response that would be most empathetic. The best responses reflect the feelings. Examples of appropriate responses are on page 158 of the Appendix. There may be more than one feeling with each statement.

1. They say that he is going to be all right!
   A. That is marvelous news.
   B. I bet you feel a lot better now.
   C. Let's go tell his sister.
   D. I'm not sure they know what they are talking about.

2. I'm tired of his ordering me around.
   A. Don't be such a wimp.
   B. He is just trying to bug you.
   C. You must be disgusted.
   D. I wouldn't put up with him if I were you.

3. You seem to understand what it's like to be left out.
   A. Yes, I've had that happen to me too.
   B. You are pleased that I understand what it is like.
   C. Everyone gets left out once in a while.
   D. But they really didn't leave you out.

4. My first check came today and I can pay what I owe him.
   A. You must be relieved to be able to pay your bill.
   B. Why are they so late in sending you your check?
   C. How did you get yourself in such a bind?
   D. Don't borrow money.

5. I'm broke. No job, no money.
  A. I know where you can get a job.
  B. Would you like to borrow a few dollars?
  C. You are just lazy.
  D. It sounds like you are pretty desperate.

6. That is the best job I have ever done.
  A. Are you proud of yourself?
  B. It sounds like you are proud of yourself.
  C. But you can even do better if you apply yourself.
  D. Did you get an A?

7. I can't believe that my mother wouldn't come when you called her.
  A. That is unbelievable.
  B. I shouldn't have called her.
  C. Why don't you call her yourself?
  D. You are really mad that she didn't come.

8. He sat down and talked to me like he had all the time in the world.
  A. You are glad that he took so much time with you.
  B. I don't understand why he hasn't done that before.
  C. He is such a busy man.
  D. I wouldn't trust him if I were you.

9. I am so sorry for her. She isn't going to graduate this year.
  A. That's what happens when you don't take your studies seriously.
  B. I wonder what she will do now.
  C. You are worried about her.
  D. Don't be sorry, she deserves it.

10. I've had it up to here with her. I hope she never comes back.

    A. Hey, give her another chance.

    B. You will never find another girlfriend as neat as she is.

    C. You are really furious at her.

    D. What did you do to make her leave?

11. I did okay on the exam this morning.

    A. You are satisfied with the test.

    B. Just wait until you get it back.

    C. If you had studied more you could have done better.

    D. I think I got an A.

12. Every time I think of what happened to her, tears come to my eyes.

    A. Don't let anyone see you cry.

    B. Yeah, that happened to me once too.

    C. I don't feel that way at all.

    D. You feel sad because of what happened.

13. I never thought I could be so calm when things went wrong.

    A. That is unusual for you, isn't it?

    B. You are content with the way you reacted.

    C. Things always seem to turn out all right.

    D. I'm going to nominate you for the cool cucumber award.

14. I'm not sure what he wants, but I think he's up to no good.

    A. I don't trust him either.

    B. You can trust him.

    C. You are apprehensive.

    D. Why don't you tell him that?

15. That teacher, I don't like her!

    A. You are certainly peeved at her.
    B. No one likes her.
    C. You don't like any of your teachers.
    D. They should fire her.

16. There is a chance I may get accepted after all.
    A. You are excited that you may get to go there.
    B. Don't be sure about that.
    C. Have you told anyone else?
    D. I wouldn't go there if I were you.

17. All right, do it your way—do anything you want.
    A. Okay, I will.
    B. Don't yell at me.
    C. It sounds like you are pretty bitter.
    D. Don't be angry.

18. Our team should have a good year.
    A. Anything would be better than last year.
    B. Only if everyone on the team stays healthy.
    C. You are pleased with the team's potential.
    D. I don't think they will.

19. He acted like I was someone important; he even remembered my name.
    A. What is your name?
    B. You are delighted that he treated you with respect.
    C. Do you think he really meant it?
    D. Do people usually have trouble with your name?

20. When I think of the money I spent on that dress, I could cry.
    A. Just take it back to the store.
    B. It really looks nice on you.
    C. You are annoyed that you spent so much on it.
    D. It sure wasn't worth it.

21. No one ever comes over. I am always alone.
    A. You feel lonely.
    B. I feel that way too sometimes.
    C. Why don't you ask Bill to come over?
    D. Don't feel that way.

22. That class is interesting. I think I'll like it after all.
    A. How could anyone like that class!
    B. You're eager about that class.
    C. Watch out. I hear that it gets pretty hard.
    D. What made you change your mind?

23. It is going to take a tremendous amount of effort but I
    know we can do it.
    A. I don't think it will be worth the effort.
    B. I'm not so sure we can.
    C. Oh, but we have failed so many times.
    D. You are enthusiastic.

You may very well ask what would happen if you guessed
the wrong feeling. What if someone told you he wanted to
die and you replied, "You feel hopeless," and that wasn't it
at all. Actually you haven't lost anything by your mistake
because the speaker will usually correct you and then
express the feeling, whatever it is. "No, I am not feeling
hopeless, I am just distressed." You have succeeded in
putting him in touch with the feeling, and that is one of the
purposes of active listening.

Carl Rogers,[1] a psychotherapist who developed a technique of counseling called client-centered therapy, described the effect of active listening:

I can testify that when you are in psychological distress
and someone really hears you without passing judg-

[1] Carl Rogers. *Freedom to Learn*. C.E. Merritt, 1969.

ment on you, without trying to take responsibility for you, without trying to mold you, it feels damn good. At these times, it has relaxed the tension in me. It has permitted me to bring out the frightening feeling, guilt, the despair, the confusions that have been a part of my experience. When I have been listened to and when I have been heard, I am able to reperceive my world in a new way and to go on. It is amazing that feelings which were completely awful, become bearable when someone listens. It is astonishing how elements which seem insolvable become solvable when someone hears; how confusions which seem irremediable turn into relatively clear flowing streams when one is understood. I have deeply appreciated the times what I have experienced this sensitive, empathic, concentrated listening.

E. AUTONOMY

People in crisis generally experience a sense of loss of power. Remember that it is the feeling response to a situation that causes the crisis, so in addition to helping someone get in touch with the feelings, it is also crucial to help him get in touch with the power he has over his own feelings. Everyone has strength and power. One of the consequences of a crisis is feeling helpless. A person who feels powerless thinks, "If I were a smarter or stronger person I could handle this. There is nothing I can do to make it better." It is taking on an attitude of being defeated.

A step toward restoring the sense of power is to help the person realize that his feelings are his and exist without outside control. Children begin to learn independence and autonomy when they first strike out on their own to do things for themselves and take pride in what they do. They also learn to be responsible for themselves. When someone is in charge and is responsible for himself he is strong and powerful. When a crisis occurs and everything seems to go wrong, he loses the sense of power, independence, and autonomy.

How can words restore autonomy? You give up power by thinking that others or something outside of yourself can control your emotions. No one else has your emotions on a puppet string. When you accuse someone else of making you angry, you are essentially saying that someone else controls your feelings. Change the words and you realize that you are angry because you choose to be. If you say, "You make me angry when you do that," you are giving away your autonomy, your independence. Change the sentence to: "I am angry when you do that." Instead of saying: "You scare me when you come home so late," rephrase it to: "I feel scared when you come home so late." This is a way of communicating that you own your feelings and are in control of yourself.

Another way of encouraging autonomy through words and communication is to use "I" messages. That brings the feeling right inside where it belongs. If you say, "The problem is overwhelming," you are not expressing how you feel. Who is overwhelmed? Is it the problem? No, it is you. To communicate the feeling of being overwhelmed, change the sentence to, "I am overwhelmed with this problem." Which of these two sentence fosters autonomy: "It is maddening when that happens," or "I get infuriated when that happens"?

F. SUMMARY

Communicating on a feeling level with someone who is experiencing a crisis lets that person know he is understood, his feeling are shared, and he is not alone with his suffering. We have usually had little practice communicating this way. There are four basic categories of feelings with different levels of intensity: happy, sad, angry, or scared. To communicate on a feeling level, it is important to separate feelings from thoughts. We often say *feel like* or *feel that* when we really are talking about a thought. Active listening is not just listening, but conveying to the speaker that you understand how he feels. There are three steps in active listening: (1) identifying the feeling; (2) accepting the feeling; and (3) reflecting the feeling. The manner of communicating can help someone get in touch with his power of autonomy. Accepting feelings as one's own can be expressed with "I" messages. Other people don't make you feel a certain way; you have an influence over the way you feel because you have a choice.

REFERENCES

Training Manual. The Suicide and Crisis Center, Dallas, Texas.

CHAPTER 6

A Model for Crisis Intervention: What to Do and What Not to Do

The empathetic communication skills described in Chapter 5 serve the purpose of helping someone in crisis by letting him know that his feelings are understood and accepted. That helps to dissipate the sense of isolation. Intervening in a crisis begins there and continues through a systematic model that leads to decision-making and a specific plan of action that will permit the person in crisis to take control of some aspect of the situation that has led to the crisis. Each step of the model has a definite purpose to progressively guide the person in crisis from turmoil and confusion to calmness and rationality. It becomes the task of the listener to learn these basic steps and incorporate the model into his helping style.

In general, each step of the model answers a question. Use these questions as guidelines for effective intervention.

1. What is he feeling?
2. What has happened?
3. What does he want to see changed?
4. How is he going to do that?

A. ESTABLISH RAPPORT

Feelings are the main topic in the first step. The technique of active listening is used to identify the feelings. That lays the foundation for the rest of the conversation. Without it, a successful resolution is much more difficult. It establishes a trust relationship between the speaker and the listener. When feelings are discussed and listened to with acceptance and respect, the sharpness, intensity, and overwhelming aspect of the emotions are reduced. The issues become more clear, and the person in crisis can reason and problem-solve more effectively. Thoughts are separated from feelings, and the listener proves he understands. The speaker is no longer isolated and alone; at last someone understands what is being felt.

B. EXPLORE THE PROBLEM

When someone in trouble asks for help from a friend, the usual response is to try to find out what is causing the problem, what has happened. Talking about the problem is much easier than talking about feelings. Most often, if the person in crisis is willing to talk, the problem comes tumbling out and the feelings are ignored or confused with a thought. Notice that in the four steps of crisis intervention, exploring the problem is the *second* step and should be put on hold until the feelings are identified by several active listening responses. Then and only then can you move on to find out what happened, what the precipitating event is.

As the conversation continues, the listener lets the person in crisis know that he has heard both the feeling and the content of what is being said. The model for this kind of reflection is "you feel...because...." "You feel angry because your father yelled at you." "You feel lost because your friend is moving 1,000 miles away." "You are dismayed because you didn't pass the exam."

What you are doing for the person in crisis is clarifying the feelings and identifying what has happened. The listener attempts to find out what situation has brought out the feelings that caused the crisis. Remember that when someone is in crisis the intense emotions make it very difficult to think rationally and be logical. You, the listener, become a psychological mirror, and that helps the speaker to sort things out and see his feelings and problems through you. You become a great asset in helping to reduce the overwhelming intensity of feelings. Now is the time for more practice.

Exercise III   Stimulus Statements II

Read the following statements. Identify the feeling and the most salient or important point in each short paragraph. Write an appropriate response of "You feel... because...." Suggested responses that promote understanding and examples of responses that would not promote understanding are found on page 159 of the Appendix.

1. I want to quit school. It's such a drag. Everyone treats me like a stupid kid. What good does it do for me to stick it out and be miserable?

2. My dad got furious when I mentioned dropping out. I brought the subject up at dinner last night and he really hit the ceiling. Then he hit me. He was so upset that he grounded me for the rest of the school year. I can't even go to the basketball games.

3. Can you imagine! I have to stay home without phone privileges for four months just because I said I didn't think I was going to pass a couple of classes this semester.

4. I will be sixteen in a couple of months. I don't care about the bruise on my face; I guess I'm used to that. But if he talks to me that way again I am tempted to take off. Besides, I don't think he would care if I left.

5. It would be so much easier to be on my own. I could get a job, a car, and my own apartment. I would not have to listen to his yelling or my mom's griping.

6. Mom is all the time telling me what to do. All she worries about is how clean my room is or how loud the music is so it won't bother Dad.

7. It is so bad around here. I don't even want to come home! How do you like that? I don't want to go to school in the morning or come home at night. Where do I belong?

8. I just don't fit into this world. Maybe I wasn't meant to be here at all. I wish I were never born.

9. I am so tired of it all. I know down deep that my

parents love me, but they have a heck of a way of showing it.

10. There is absolutely nothing I can do to change anything. I have tried everything I can think of and nothing works.

11. They just don't understand. No one understands. Nobody sees me as me. I feel so alone.

C. FOCUS

In this third step of the crisis intervention model, the person in crisis is now ready to decide what change he wants to see happen. Sometimes this becomes quite a challenge, because a person in crisis often has many stressful things happening in a short period of time. Attempting to solve them all at one time is not productive. Trying to bring about change without knowing what change is wanted is like starting out on a trip without knowing your destination. The person in crisis, with the guidance of the listener, picks one thing to focus on first. It should be something that is causing emotional pain, and there should be some reason to believe it can successfully be solved.

Jim was a junior in high school when his dad and mom separated. Jim's ten-year-old sister stayed with his mother and Jim moved into an apartment with his dad. One of the reasons he wanted to live with his dad was the promise of a car for his next birthday, and the idea of an apartment with no lawn to mow was appealing. Jim's father traveled a lot with his business, so Jim had the responsibility of using his time constructively after school and in the evening without the supervision of an adult. Jim looked forward to the freedom and anticipated a comfortable home without the constant arguing and bickering. But he was surprised to find out how strange it seemed without his little sister and mom around. He had difficulty adjusting to the new living arrangement. There was still conflict between his parents. Each parent seemed to unload and dump on him. Things didn't get better as he had hoped. They only got worse.

Jim's father and mother both were encouraging him to plan to attend college after he graduated from high school. Jim began to think of marrying his girlfriend, Kathy, and looking for a job instead. They had been dating ever since the beginning of high school, and Kathy had been a tremendous support for him through his parents' separation and divorce. His grades had slipped this last year, and his interest in pursuing an academic career was not very high. Jim's folks liked Kathy but were adamantly opposed to the seriousness of the relationship. They were quick to point out that it would be most difficult for Jim to have a respectable career and make something of himself without a college degree. Whenever Jim saw his mom, their conversation turned into argument, so he began to avoid going over to the house. Then Kathy learned that her father had been transferred to another city and the family would be moving at the end of this school year. Jim was overwhelmed and felt confused and angry. He was in crisis.

Jim was facing many difficulties, none of which would be easy to solve. When Kathy told him the bad news, he found himself feeling anxious and panicky and did not know where to turn or what to do. The thought of losing Kathy was too much to bear. A crisis counselor would help Jim focus on one of his problems by asking which of them was giving him the most difficulty at this time and what would be the one thing he would most like to change. It could be his relationship with his parents, or making a decision about what to do after high school, or deciding what to do about seeing Kathy when her family moved away.

As a good listener, the crisis intervenor continues to use empathetic responses as he explores which problem to tackle first. A word of caution is in order. If Jim brings up situations that occurred many years previously, such as the death of an uncle to whom he was very close, do not choose to focus on that event. Crisis intervention deals with the here and now. Jim is in a crisis because something happened recently. Losses suffered in early childhood may affect the way Jim responds or adjusts and makes decisions as a teenager, because past experiences shape the coping (adjusting) behavior of the present. However, Jim's intense anger and confusion are a result of his current situation, and to find relief from those tensions it is necessary to focus of one part of the current situation.

D. SEEK ALTERNATIVES

When someone is in crisis it is difficult for him or her to explore creative options. Thinking becomes constricted, and only one alternative may come to mind. This is called tunnel vision. It is as though the person wore blinders and could only see the one solution straight ahead. Sometimes suicide is that one option. Suicide is always one way to make the pain go away, to end the misery that comes from emotional turmoil. There are other options, other alternatives, and during this part of the crisis intervention model it is time to see what the other solutions may be.

Everyone develops a style of solving problems as they learn to handle stress while growing up. This coping style becomes a part of the personality and is a way of adjusting to the setbacks, the pitfalls, the pressures that are unavoidable. One person may like to seclude himself and think the matter over without interference or distraction from others. A walk on the beach, sitting beside a stream in the woods, or closing the door to his room with music blaring may offer the seclusion that is sought. Someone else may learn the calming skill of meditation, which clears the mind through concentration. Still another person may find that turning to a friend or family member to talk things over may help to put things in order. Some people find that what works best for them is to avoid confrontation, to withdraw from conflict, and to accommodate to the wishes of others, which keeps a relationship peaceful. Physical activity helps some to vent the anger inside. A game of tennis or racquet ball becomes the outlet to alleviate the pent-up energy. Coping mechanisms may include professional help or even seeking a diversion in new interests or hobbies.

Some coping styles are maladaptive: They tend to help the person out of the immediate crisis situation but create other problems in the process. Turning to psychoactive drugs or alcohol as an escape is an example. Relief from tension and an initial sense of well-being accompany the use of mind-altering or mood-elevating substances. All psychoactive drugs can lead to psychological dependence, and many are physically addictive. Learning to become a responsible adult comes during the teenage years. Heavy use of drugs not only leads to dependence but destroys the opportunity to mature, to move on to the next stage of development—young adulthood and independence.

When David's dad was out of work for several months, the family faced eviction because the bills could not be paid. The immediate concern was buying food. David wrote a check with insufficient funds in the bank. This act could be considered maladaptive in that it is not accepted by the rules of society and the expectation is that society and its laws will punish the behavior. However, it was coping in some fashion. It did solve the immediate crisis.

Before a plan of action can be chosen in the last stage of crisis intervention, the available resources should be explored. By this time, if active listening has been used, the intensity and sharpness of the feelings have been reduced. Logic and reason begin to reappear. The conversation can turn toward what has been done in the past when faced with a problem. Remembering that she eventually managed okay the last time a steady boyfriend broke off may give hope that the empty, drained feelings won't last forever. Also remembering that a special aunt was a big help then can trigger a decision to make a telephone call or pay a visit to her.

If you push too quickly to find what resources are available and insist on a plan of action before the person in crisis is ready to make decisions, it may be better to go back to the active listening in the first part of the model for a while. Let the person lead you, and when it is time you will be able to sense that it is now okay to put together a specific, step-by-step outline of what to do to work through the crisis. If suicide had been an option, now is the time to encourage him to try these other options that have been thought out together. Suicide is always available. No one can take that option away.

This model of crisis intervention is used daily by counselors at crisis centers around the country. It is not magic although it works magically, particularly when talking with someone in a critical crisis. These skills can be a tremendous asset to anyone who wishes to improve his ability to communicate.

E. DOS AND DON'TS OF CRISIS INTERVENTION

Do be willing to get involved

No one wants to be a busybody or a prying neighbor, and it may be difficult to know when it would be appropriate to step forward and offer help. Sometimes a person who is suicidal may be sending out signals in hope that someone will notice that they are distress signals. Believe and trust your suspicions. Show interest and support. If any of the warning signs are present, it is time to offer assistance. There is a risk that the assistance may be refused. On the other hand, hearing the cry for help and being willing to get involved may bring the attention that is hoped for.

Don't warn or threaten

Our immediate reaction to the thought of a friend wanting to commit suicide is no! "No, I don't want you to die!" "No, you can't do that!" Refrain from expressing this reaction by warning or threatening: "If you do that, you'll be sorry." It is not illegal to attempt suicide, so threatening that he will be arrested and put in jail simply isn't true. Trying to convince him of the consequence of that action may be fruitless if the crisis has caused such intense emotions. Urging a suicidal teenager to think about the effect of his death on his parents and friends doesn't alleviate the pain or confusion of crisis. The attempt to divert attention to others may only foster guilt and shame. One of the objectives of crisis intervention is to keep the attention focused on the person in crisis so he will come to understand that he really is important and someone does care.

Do ask!

Asking a direct question about suicidal intentions does not cause someone to be suicidal. It will not plant the seed in anyone's mind. If the warning signs are there, you can bet he has already thought about suicide and is giving it consideration. Often a suicidal person has no one to listen to his scary, desperate feelings. A sense of isolation is common. The question should be straightforward. Say the word *suicide* or *die* or *kill*. It is important to convey your willingness to be open and direct. If he trusts that you will not respond with anger or ridicule, he will most likely respond with honesty. Do not say, "You are not thinking of suicide, are you?" More helpful is a question like, "Do you want to die?" Instead of suggesting the idea of suicide, your question offers a source of relief. You set yourself up as a person who is willing to listen. The worst thing that could come from a direct question, if you are wrong in interpreting the clues, is some embarrassment.

Do be willing to listen

If you truly are interested in helping, offering a listening ear will affirm feelings that, in turn, affirm the person. Often the suicidal person perceives himself to be isolated and alone. He may have a family and friends and yet still think of himself as misunderstood and unloved. In this active society and in busy homes, it is the quality of interaction that is important. It takes effort and time to stop and listen and really hear what is happening. It may not be easy to hear a friend talk about dying. You may be tempted to change the subject or avoid a conversation about problems, pain, or unhappiness by telling him that you don't want to hear him say that. Yet allowing a friend to talk about what is on his mind and what he is feeling will help break that sense of isolation. Be careful not to dominate the conversation or come forth with a barrage of questions so that you give the impression of an interrogation. There should be a balance of listening and talking, a give and take. Do not reminisce about when you had a similar experience; that puts the attention on you instead of your friend. Use the empathetic active listening skills you learned in Chapter 5.

Do be a nonjudgmental listener

When you have your own firm beliefs about suicide, you may be tempted to share them, thinking that a suicidal friend may adopt your attitude and choose to live. Your belief system may include the idea that suicide is a sin and that someone who commits suicide will not be accepted by God and have eternal life. For some, this concept may indeed be sufficient to keep them alive when they desire to cease living. For others, the pain may be so great that even this thought is not as frightening as thinking that life will always be a living hell. Avoid words like *should, have to, right, wrong, good,* or *bad.* ("You should not think that way." "You have to think of others." "Suicide is wrong." "How could you even consider such a thing?") Your role as a helper is to accept the feelings and allow full expression, even if you do not approve or would not consider it yourself.

Don't promote guilt

Don't ask if he has thought how much grief suicide would cause the family and friends or tell him that suicide is a sin. Both of these issues may in fact be true for the person who is contemplating suicide, but someone in crisis is in a sense very selfish; the pain is so great that it is difficult to imagine anything more important than getting rid of it. The emphasis of the conversation needs to be kept on the feelings and the person feeling them, not on anyone or anything else. The suicidal person does not need guilt added to the already intense emotions. Avoid statements like. "Have you thought how your mother would feel?" Sometimes religious beliefs or the thought that the suicidal act would be devastating to the family are sufficient to prevent someone from killing himself. On the other hand, if you ask the question it may sound as if you haven't really been listening to what has been said about despair and hopelessness. When asking about suicide, you may hear reasons why suicide wouldn't be considered when searching for solutions; the grieving family and religion may be the reasons why.

Don't dare him to do it

This kind of reverse psychology simply doesn't work, and it could be very dangerous. There is something about proving yourself in response to a dare that can be very risky. A freshman at college took his life after his girlfriend told him he didn't have the guts to commit suicide. He was despondent because she wanted to break up. She became impatient and disgusted when he continued to plead with her not to leave. She viewed the suicide threat as a ploy to keep her as his girlfriend and had no idea that he would act on his threat. She had no intention of being callous. The suicide that followed was a tragedy.

Do remove easy access to lethal weapons or drugs

Young people are sometimes impulsive and may act
on a decision that is not carefully weighed and thought
out. A loaded gun in the drawer or supplies of sleeping
pills or potent prescription drugs in the medicine
cabinet are an invitation to dangerous, spur-of-the-
moment acts for someone who may be suicidal. It
is not that unusual for a suicide attempt to follow
the ingestion of alcohol or drugs that lower the inhi-
bitions. A study at the Dallas Suicide and Crisis
Center showed that 60 percent of teenagers who
killed themselves had alcohol in their blood. That
does not mean they were alcoholic, but it does indicate a depressed nervous system and lowering of
protective defenses. Removing guns and pills from
the home is a form of protection and can very well be
done with the knowledge of the suicidal person. It
gives a caring message that you are concerned and
want to help your friend protect himself. Again, this is
not your choice alone. Family and close friends can
form a protective shield. Suicide is a cry for help, for
attention. Respond with that attention. The hope is
that emotional needs can be communicated in other
ways and suicide no longer seem the only alternative.

Don't give advice

The Earl of Chesterfield is quoted as saying in 1748:
"Advice is seldom welcome; and those who want it
most always like it least." When someone in crisis
pleads to be told what to do, that is not really what is
being asked. One of the basic assumptions of crisis
theory is the matter of control. The person in crisis
perceives himself as not being in control of what is

happening around him or to him. If you respond
to the request for advice by giving advice, you are
buying into that fallacy. You are in essence saying that
you agree that he has to be told what to do. That
conveys disrespect. How often when advice is offered
it is followed with a million reasons why it won't work.
Counselors label this as "Yes, but..." "Yes, but if I
tell her that, she will be even more furious at me and I
will be worse off than I am now." "Yes, but if I tell my
parents I am pregnant they will never forgive me. I
want to handle this alone." Pretty soon it seems like
you are beating your head against a brick wall. It is not
the role of a crisis intervenor to come up with the
alternatives and solutions. Your role is to be there, to
listen to the intense feelings, and to give a message of
caring and understanding. That is the magic of the
model of crisis intervention. Once these feelings are
shared and heard, they are relieved. Then seeking
solutions and alternatives becomes an easier task.
You can help clarify what alternatives there may be,
but avoid coming up with all of them yourself. Show
respect. Do not give advice.

Don't try to cheer him up
It is difficult to see someone we love in pain, physical
or emotional. When a friend is in crisis and shows
symptoms of depression, you may be tempted to try
to take away the sadness. Making jokes or creating
diversions may bring a smile, but most likely it will
be at your kind attempts and not really because the
sadness is relieved. Such efforts show our own discomfort when we see someone else hurting and are an
outlet for our own emotion. We don't want someone
else to be sad: We might become sad also, so we are

only taking care of our own needs. It's okay to be sad, it's okay to be angry, it's okay to be afraid. When these feelings are intense, relief is sought, and a friend is in a good position to help bring that relief—but not by becoming a clown, treating the seriousness lightly, or trying to divert attention from the hurt. The emotions of sadness and happiness are incompatible. The smiles will come when the tears disappear.

Don't allow yourself to be sworn to secrecy
When a friend asks you not to tell anyone else what she is going to tell you, you may readily agree as a gesture of your close friendship. It indicates that there is a bond between you, and there is a sense of warmth and security from that kind of a relationship. However, if that friend proceeds to tell you that she is considering killing herself, it is one of the few incidences when you absolutely must break that promise. That is too heavy a load for you to carry by yourself, and it is time to call in the troops, to mobilize forces with parents and friends who can bring the attention and help that is needed. Your friend may think she has been betrayed and be irritated at you, but that is a small price to pay for helping someone live. If it is possible, the best way out is not to promise to keep it a secret in the first place. Qualify your agreement and say honestly that you want to keep the conversation confidential but without knowing what the topic is, you really can't promise that.

Do get help from other friends, family members, or persons or agencies specializing in crisis intervention and suicide prevention. Learn what resources are available in your area for young people. Most communities have places that specialize in offering help for pregnancy, drug abuse, and so on. An excellent school project would be to find out their location, telephone number, and the services they provide even before they are needed in time of crisis.

F. SUMMARY

This chapter has given a basic outline of crisis intervention in four steps: (1) establish rapport and trust with active listening; (2) explore the problem and recent happenings; (3) focus on one aspect of the situation and work on that aspect for now; and (4) review resources and together seek a plan of action.

Principles to follow in suicide prevention by helping someone in crisis involve using his strengths and discovering the control he has over what is happening:

1. Be aware. Learn the warning signs.
2. Get involved. Become available. Show interest and support.
3. Ask if he or she is thinking about suicide.
4. Be direct. Talk openly and freely about suicide.
5. Be willing to listen. Allow expression of feelings. Accept the feelings. Don't tell him or her to feel better.
6. Be nonjudgmental. Don't debate whether suicide is right or wrong, or feelings are good or bad. Don't lecture on the value of life.
7. Don't dare him or her to do it.
8. Don't give advice by making decisions for someone else or tell him or her to behave differently.
9. Don't ask why. That encourages defensiveness.
10. Offer empathy, not sympathy.

11. Don't act shocked. That will put distance between you.
12. Don't be sworn to secrecy. Seek support.
13. Offer hope that alternatives are available but do not offer glib reassurance. It only proves you don't understand.
14. Take action. Remove means. Get help from persons or agencies specializing in crisis intervention and suicide prevention.

PART ◇ IV

WHEN IT HURTS

CHAPTER 7

Coping with Depression

Juan stood in the middle of the busy entrance to the psychiatric emergency room at a large county hospital with tears running down his face. His shoulders were stooped and his chin touched his chest. His movements were slow, and he gave the appearance of being in a confused dream world. He couldn't remember when he hadn't felt unhappy and depressed. The school psychologist had helped his family realize the seriousness and danger of his situation, and two days earlier his mother had made an appointment for him at the counseling clinic. Juan knew that his family could not afford even the small fee that would be charged for the help that everyone said he needed. His father was lucky to have a steady job, but there were six brothers and sisters at home and one paycheck never seemed to stretch far enough. How could Juan justify using some of that money when the car needed repair, the utility company had threatened twice in the last year to cut off the gas for heating, and he knew that the doctor still had not been paid for treating his little sister when she was hospitalized with pneumonia.

A flurry of activity drew Juan's attention from the woman behind the counter who was asking him questions about his age and about his family. The paramedics wheeled in a man whose shirt was covered with blood. Juan wondered how much it hurt to be shot in the chest. Only a few minutes (or was it hours?) before, Juan had held a gun to his heart. Life was too painful. He could think of no reason for living. His family would be better off without him. Last night his girlfriend had hinted that she wanted to date someone else. He had thought of her most of the sleepless night and of the dreams they had together. He hadn't handed in his English assignment this morning, and his teacher had told him he was in danger of flunking. He was afraid he would not be promoted to the ninth grade. He was tall for his age, and many people said he looked more like eighteen years old than fourteen. How could he stay in middle school for another year? His mother wanted him to be the first in his family to get a high school diploma, but that dream seemed impossible to him now. He would be so humiliated, and his mother would be ashamed of him. He really did not want to die. He just did not want to live with this suffering anymore.

It was easy to buy a gun on the street. Almost as easy as it was to buy drugs. He had tried to erase his depression by smoking a little pot, but all that had done was make him feel worse. He was smart enough to realize that drugs weren't the answer. He had had the gun in his pocket at school when his teacher had told him that his counselor wanted to see him. Instead of going directly to the counselor's office, he stopped in the boys' restroom. Once he was alone he had taken the gun out of his pocket and held it in his hand. That was when Richard had walked in. He couldn't remember much about what had happened next. All he knew now was that the school security guard and his counselor were with him as he stood at the admitting desk at the hospital. He wondered what he would tell his mother when she arrived. He did not understand it himself, so how was he going to explain it to his family and the doctors. At least he had been stopped from shooting himself, and for that he was thankful.

Juan was fortunate that his school counselor had recognized his depression and known he needed help. Having a gun in school is a serious offense, and he could have been expelled. His poor grades could have been attributed to a lack of motivation. It is hard to believe that a child as young as Juan could be experiencing a malaise that for so long has been considered an adult problem. When Juan's case was examined, the physicians and counselors realized that he had been depressed for several years. It was difficult to pinpoint exactly when it all began. His parents remembered him as a smiling, happy youngster but didn't think too much of it when be became moody and angry at home. They just thought he was turning into a typical teenager, with harder subjects at school and more serious decisions to make about his future.

A. RECOGNIZING DEPRESSION

Depression manifests itself differently in children than in adults. Most adults know what it is to feel sad and in a bad mood. It is hard to eat regularly or sleep soundly. A feeling of hopelessness and weepiness prevails. They have little energy and feel physically tired and sluggish. They may become irritable and snap at people. It seems like a hopeless situation when one is trapped and can do nothing about it.

Children, on the other hand, may or may not exhibit

these symptoms. Even if they have trouble sleeping and eating, their parents are not likely to attribute it to depression. Somewhat more confusing is the fact that a depressed child may become fussy, hyperactive, bored, or restless and get into trouble frequently. Parents and teachers can become exasperated with this kind of acting-out behavior if they do not understand the nature of masked depression.

Depressed teenagers may exhibit symptoms similar to those of younger children or those of adults. Their behavior may be seen as that of a rebellious teenager. Symptoms of adolescent depression include:

Lack of concern for personal hygiene and appearance

Restlessness or grouchiness

Hostility and aggression

Desire to run away

Belief that no one understands them

Failure to get along with siblings or parents

Withdrawal from family and social activities

Sensitivity to rejection

Fluctuating moods

Loss or gain in weight

Fatigue

Self-reproach or self-depreciation

Diminished ability to concentrate

Thoughts of suicide and dying

B. KINDS OF DEPRESSION

Adolescence is a developmental period when emotions normally take a roller coaster ride. So many hormonal and physical changes occur in such a short time that it takes some getting used to the new body and new image. Sadness or depressed feelings occur in almost everyone at one time or another. It doesn't necessarily indicate mental illness. Normal "blue moods" may be a reaction to disappointments or, for a girl, the approach of her menstrual period.

Reactive depression goes beyond the normal mood shifts. The sad feelings are tied to specific events or circumstances, usually a response to a loss of some kind. The depression is a physiological response to stress. Some people seem to be predisposed to stress. A few of the common losses that trigger depression in adolescents are the following:

Moves When a family is transferred to another part of the country after Mom or Dad gets a better job, or when a family moves to another part of town to a bigger home or a less expensive apartment, there is a big adjustment for the children. It is not easy to make a whole new set of friends and get used to a new school. It takes time to find a place in a group or get involved in extracurricular activities.

Graduation This is a milestone in anyone's life. It is a window of time that opens out to more responsibilities and independence. Graduation is a time to celebrate academic accomplishments and close friendships. It also means breaking up some of those friendships as people move away to college or jobs elsewhere. Life won't be so structured anymore. With freedom from class schedules come choices of what to do. And believe it or not, many young people do miss their old high school and grieve the loss of their childhood.

Failure   Hurt pride, shame, and embarrassment all may trigger reactive depression. Not being chosen homecoming queen, not making the football team, not passing a course, not being accepted by a prestigious college all may not seem serious to an adult. However, it is not easy to feel good about yourself when you perceive yourself as a failure, and attempts to cheer you up don't really help. Failure to fulfill a dream or meet expectations of parents, teachers, or yourself can hurt deeply

Chronic illness   The loss of health and ability to do what the rest of the kids can do is hard to take. Longing to be able to get out of bed or wheelchair, to participate in sports, to stay out late with friends makes it difficult to keep up good spirits. The precious years of childhood and youth can be lost to the struggle for survival. Nothing takes precedent over the road to recovery or at least rehabilitation to regain some measure of health. Emotional well-being can affect how successful the recovery can be.

Breakup of a relationship   Self-esteem and hopes for the future may be tied up in a love relationship. With the loss of a girlfriend or boyfriend it may be difficult to imagine ever being happy again. So much is tied up in being identified as "belonging" to that special someone. It can be a real blow to the self-image. This grief is similar to the sadness felt when parents separate or some close dies. It seems as though the world is coming to an end. This pain may be quite physical as well as emotional. Time helps, as it does in getting over other kinds of distressful losses.

Normal moodiness and reactive depression are two kinds of depression. If the symptoms persist over several months and cannot be linked to any specific event or circumstance, it is then called chronic or clinical depression. Chronically depressed people are not that way because they are lazy, lack willpower, are goofing off, or are seeking sympathy and attention. An actual chemical change takes place when the depression is this severe. A reduction in nerve transmitters in the central nervous system makes it difficult for information to be relayed from one neuron (nerve cell) to another. Serotonin and norepinephrine are neurotransmitters linked to depression. They are the chemical messengers that carry the signals between the neurons. Depression results when there is an insufficient amount of these chemicals in the brain. For unknown reasons, females are more apt to develop depression than males. Some people seem to be more predisposed than others to these chemical deficiencies. This predisposition may be inherited.

Depression can also be a psychiatric illness. It can become so severe that a person is almost totally incapacitated. He or she can no longer function in school or work. Daily living becomes impossible, and the person may have to be hospitalized. Long-lasting depression is not normal, and, as we have seen in Chapter 3, depression can lead to suicidal behavior. It is dangerous to ignore the seriousness of depression. Adults need to realize that young people can become depressed and that the symptoms may be different from what adults experience. Young people need to know that depression can be treated and that they can win the battle with their emotions.

C. TREATING DEPRESSION

Depression will not last forever. As much as you may think it will never go away, it eventually does. That doesn't mean you should simply wait for it to disappear. You are not so helpless or powerless as to allow the discomfort to continue to pull you down into the mire of gloom. There are positive steps you can take to speed up your recovery. There are also things teens do to cover up the depression that may only deepen it and complicate their recovery. Alcohol and drugs both cause depression and are symptoms of it. Drugs may also mask the signs of depression, making it difficult to recognize.

Brenda's teachers became concerned when she was frequently absent during the last six-week grading period. The absences were erratic; often only the first or last class was skipped. When she did come, she often fell asleep at her desk and seemed irritable and cross with both her friends and the faculty. She had been an above average student, but now she was failing most of her classes. Her parents were in the process of obtaining a divorce, and everyone knew she was having a rough time. It was assumed that when things settled down at home she would become her congenial self again. One day she complained of not feeling well and was sent to the nurse's office. The nurse suspected she was under the influence of alcohol and called her mother to come to school. Brenda described her drinking as a way to ease the tension and sadness she was feeling. It gave her an initial sense of relief and even euphoria. In a way, she was trying to medicate herself, but it was only a temporary escape. Alcohol is a depressant and only deepened her sense of despair. She had lost interest in her friends and her schoolwork and was headed down a path of self-destruction. Brenda entered a residential treatment center and then continued her recovery with an outpatient support group for over a year. The addiction had to be treated before the underlying depression could be addressed. She eventually learned to deal with the separation of her parents and, with the help of her therapists, found a way to be free of the depression.

One of the things you feel when you are depressed is a compelling desire to do nothing. However, a way to cope with this lack of energy is to do the opposite of what you feel like doing. Physical exercise actually creates more energy. A brisk walk, a robust session of aerobics or workout, or an invigorating game of tennis stimulates the body. It does more than make you physically tired. It helps you to feel better emotionally. Sometimes a stimulating shower and change of clothes or fresh makeup may perk you up. The hardest part is to talk yourself into doing something that takes energy when you think you don't have any. When you are battling depression make sure to schedule physical exercise into your daily routine.

If you ask ten people what they do to cheer themselves up during a particularly stressful time, you probably will get ten different answers. Stacy likes to go to the mall and browse in the stores, Jim treats himself to a gourmet ice cream cone, Betty calls a friend who moved away and whom she misses very much, Gerald calls the teenline. No one thing works for everyone. A change of pace helps change a perspective or attitude. Try something different or something that you enjoyed doing in the past. Maybe a change of scenery with a visit to a relative or old friend will get you going again. Don't push yourself, or you will only feel more frustrated; but eventually you will hit upon a way to cope with normal mood shifts.

Depression seems to be seasonal. There is a theory that our affect or mood is affected by the amount and duration of sunshine. Some advocate increasing the inside lighting to compensate for the long hours of darkness during the winter months. We have all heard about "holiday blues." Depression is more prevalent at Christmas (although the incidence of suicide does not increase at this time). Childhood memories of wonder and magic and happiness can bring disillusionment if the family is no longer together or has suffered financial difficulties. Celebrating Christmas in a different way or building in plenty of time for yourself during this hectic season can alleviate the let-down or frazzled feelings.

If the depression is a reaction to an event that caused you to grieve or mourn, you will have to work to overcome it. Grief is the normal yearning for whatever or whomever you lost. It is important to let yourself experience the pain before you can heal. Once you allow yourself to grieve and time elapses after your loss, you can better adjust to life without the person you miss or to the failure to attain an important goal. Eventually you will be able to reinvest your attention and attraction in another relationship or set your sights on another reasonable goal. You will have learned something about your capabilities and how to choose goals for yourself that will be challenging but attainable. To protect yourself from the hurt of failure, you can choose alternative goals in the first place. If your first choice goes down the tubes you have something to fall back on and can still come out a winner.

One of the best ways to cope with depression is to rely on good friends to support you as you recover. Most people have not learned how to be good listeners. The skills described in Chapter 5 are mastered by only a few. Good friends may want to help you but may not know how to break the wall around you. You will need to search for a friend or maybe a teacher who is empathic and willing to listen to your feelings. Avoid someone who tends to preach, or it may heighten your sense of being a burden and a failure. Find someone who will not tell you to snap out of it. A special listener is one who is willing to hear your feelings and let you talk it out. He is encouraging and accepting. He is there when you need him and still gives you space so that he will not intrude or foster too much dependence.

So far we have talked about how to cope with normal or short episodes of depression. If the symptoms continue for more than a couple of weeks you may wish to seek professional help. Depression is one of the most common complaints of those who seek counseling or therapy. It is also one of the most successfully treated. We have talked about a physical change that accompanies serious changes in mood: a deficiency in chemical neurotransmitters in the brain. Chemotherapy or treatment with medicine can increase the levels of transmitters in the central nervous system or can prevent the chemicals in the space between the nerve endings (synaptic canals) from being reabsorbed, leaving more of the chemicals available to alleviate depression. Once treatment begins, it takes several days for positive effects to occur. There can also be uncomfortable side effects such as drowsiness, constipation, or dry mouth. A physician must prescribe and monitor the medication. If a well-meaning friend offers to share antidepressant medication, do not even sample it. Never take anyone else's prescription. Trust your own physician to find the right kind and right dosage just for you.

A counselor or psychotherapist will also be a significant part of any treatment plan to combat depression. You may wish to consult a psychiatrist, who is a medical doctor and thus can prescribe drugs. Or you may turn to a psychologist, who also has a doctoral degree but must have a physician prescribe medicine for you if you need it. A licensed counselor should also be able to help you. You may wish to ask your school counselor to refer you to an agency or a private clinic. The crisis centers listed in the Appendix have lists of referrals in your community. It is important for you to be comfortable with whomever you ask for help. Ask them to explain what kind of services you can expect. Counselors and therapists have different ideas about how to treat depression depending on their training and experience. They will be willing to describe their credentials and explain which counseling theories they follow if you inquire. Fees may vary from agency to agency. Private therapists also differ in what they charge for their services. Many community agencies and therapists work on a sliding scale, which means they charge a lower fee to clients who cannot afford to pay the regular charge. There should be help for everyone who needs it regardless of ability to pay.

D. SUMMARY

Young people can feel depressed as well as adults. The symptoms may differ, but the disruption in daily living is similar. The most common feelings are hopelessness, irritability, sadness, fatigue, aggressiveness, worthlessness, and boredom. Difficulty in sleeping and eating is common. Problems occur in school and with friendships. Parents may attribute the changes to normal adolescence and a lack of motivation or rebellion, when in fact the depression inhibits normal functioning. The "blues" are normal, and shifts in moods can be expected in everyone from time to time. A traumatic event or loss can trigger reactive depression that will diminish with time. If no problem or loss has occurred and if the depression lasts longer than expected, it is called chronic or clinical depression. Professional help may be considered when it is this severe. Counselors will recommend an active approach with physical exercise and changes in routine. The support of friends is also important. When the depression is so deep that it is immobilizing, it could be a major mood disorder and could even require hospitalization. There have been significant developments in the last couple of decades in the treatment of depression. Chemotherapy has given hope to thousands of people who before would have had to conquer their despair with time and continuing pain alone.

E. TEST YOURSELF ON DEPRESSION

Because the symptoms of depression are sometimes difficult to recognize and can take many forms, this treatable and common illness often goes undetected. The following brief test is not meant to be conclusive by itself. If you answer "yes" to two or more of the questions you may consider consulting a physician or mental health professional.

		Yes	No
1.	I am disappointed in myself.	___	___
2.	I have difficulty concentrating or remembering things.	___	___
3.	I sometimes feel anxious or irritable for no apparent reason.	___	___
4.	I think that my future is hopeless and I can do nothing about it.	___	___
5.	I have difficulty sleeping at night and staying awake during the day.	___	___
6.	I have lost my appetite.	___	___
7.	I really don't feel well most of the time.	___	___
8.	I think I am unattractive.	___	___

9. I have lost interest in friends and other
   social activities.   ___ ___
10. I often feel like crying.   ___ ___

REFERENCES

William Worden. *Grief Counseling and Grief Therapy*. Springer, 1982.

Ari Kiev. *Recovery from Depression*. Dutton, 1980.

Philip Patros and Tonia Shamoo. *Depression and Suicide in Children and Adolescents*. Allyn and Bacon, 1989.

PART V

AFTER A SUICIDE

CHAPTER 8

Surviving the Loss:

Grief and Growth

Suicide can be described as an interpersonal act. It is killing oneself, yet it also kills part of everyone who is close to or loves the person who dies. The emotional pain for the suicide victim is over, but it is only beginning for the survivors. If you have had a friend or family member commit suicide, you will be able to identify the sharp and long-lasting feelings that arise with grief. These emotions are similar to those felt while mourning any violent, unexpected death. Unfortunately, additional reactions occur when that violent, unexpected death is a suicide. The feelings themselves can be scary. The most frightening aspect is not knowing what to expect and being told trite platitudes in an attempt to cheer you up and "take away" the negative grief feelings. Those feelings, as scary and awful as they are, have to be experienced and worked through for the grief to subside. The process will continue until satisfactory adjustments are achieved and firmly established. It is a growth experience in the direction of maturity.

The process is called grief work, and indeed it is strenuous work. How many times have you heard, "Time heals all wounds"? In the case of grief, time helps, but time alone won't heal. *You* have to put some effort into the struggle to come out a winner. And don't believe anyone who tells you that the time spent mourning after a suicide should be limited to three months or six months or nine months. This is one case in which you need to give yourself permission to take a long time—as long as it takes. It would not be unusual for some aspects of mourning to continue for two years or more.

It may be disheartening to learn that it can take such a long time. You may wonder how in the world you are going to be able to stand it. First of all, however, the pain does not stay as sharp as it was in the beginning, and it may even go away for periods of time. On the other hand, it may bring a sense of relief to know it is okay to cry all over again when something reminds you of your loss and the untimely death. The void will always be there with a memory, and for that reason some say mourning is never complete. The comfort and hope come as life becomes different and the void no longer dominates your being. You will never be able to go back to life as it was before. If all goes well you will be able to recover, but you will be different. As you can learn from experiencing a crisis and having the opportunity for growth, so will you learn from a grief experience. The painful lesson is learning to face and survive a loss.

A. THE EXPECTED AND UNEXPECTED FEELINGS

Shock   The first emotional reaction is a numbness that comes with the realization that a loved one has died. This shock will serve to protect you for a few days so you can manage to participate in the funeral service and receive traditional expressions of sympathy from neighbors and friends. The suicide may have been unanticipated as in a sudden accident where there has been no opportunity for preparatory grief or to say goodbye. The wave of cold shock may sweep over you even if you had some warning. The disbelief wards off the fear of its becoming true. "I didn't think he really would go through with it." The possibility that it may happen is denied. When it does happen, it is a tremendous blow. The body reels and the head swims in a fog and daze. The shock walls off the gut-wrenching depth of emotions that must surface later.

Sadness   This is the emotion that is most often associated with grief and mourning. It is sorrow, it is woe. It is a longing, and yearning, and emptiness. The sadness saps the energy, prevents sleep, takes away the appetite, and robs you of the joy of life. This depression may last for several months, or it may lift after a few weeks. For some, tears and sobbing express this emotion. Others are unable to cry or even talk about it. If the suicide comes after a period of turmoil and unhappiness for you and the deceased, instead of sadness you may experience relief. You no longer are burdened with worry, and you may even feel relief because the pain is over for the one who died. It is over. The worry and tension are dissipated, and the flood of other emotions simply may not happen.

Fear   One of the myths that surround suicide is the idea
that it is inheritable. If one of your family commits suicide,
it does not mean that that will also be your fate. Suicide is
not transmitted genetically. There is, however, evidence
that a predisposition to a chemical imbalance that causes
depression may be inherited. This can be treated successfully with drugs. Unnecessary fear may be generated if
you accept the myth that you will inevitably develop self-
destructive tendencies if someone else in your family has
died by suicide.

If the person who committed suicide was a parent, you
may be tremendously worried about the support you will
need until you become more independent. The anxiety
and helpless feelings reflect the question of whether you
can get along by yourself.

If the suicide victim was a close friend, you may fear that
you will never recover from your grief and always feel the
void and emptiness inside you.

Another source of fear stems from a lack of understanding
of the grief process. If this is the first loss you have suffered, you may think you are experiencing a mental break-
down. Seeing or hearing the dead person talking to you
does not mean you are going crazy. It can be frightening
or, for some, a soothing experience.

Shame   Although attitudes toward suicide have changed
throughout history and vary from culture to culture, a
stigma of disgrace is still prevalent against the surviving
family of a suicide victim. Some judge suicide a sin, a sign
of weakness, or mental illness. Actions of a family reflect
on one another. You are proud of each other's accomplishments and ashamed of each other's failures. If suicide
is regarded as failure, the family may share the embarrassment of the act. Unfortunately, that shame may prevent

you from expresing your grief to others or talking about the circumstances of the death. The same thing can happen to friends and neighbors. They do not know what to say either, and they avoid offering the usual support and sympathy to the grieving family. Thus, shame can hinder and prolong the grief process.

Anger Janet's family reeled under the pain after her father killed himself. She herself was extremely angry to have been left with such horrible pain because he had chosen to leave her. It was not fair that she be so tormented. Her father was an alcoholic and had been unable to support he family for over a year. Her mother had worked since Janet's brother had started school, and Janet was made responsible for most of the household chores. She did not have time to participate in any after-school activities because she was expected to come home and take care of her little brother—and protect him from the wrath of her father when he was in an alcoholic rage. Janet loved her father very much when he was sober. When he was not drinking he was kind and gentle, and she spent many hours playing golf or walking in the woods with him. He was an excellent golfer, and Janet was hoping to make golf her career. Her dad encouraged her to become a professional, which had always been his secret desire.

Now he was dead. He had chosen to die. Janet thought her dad had rejected her when he committed suicide, and she responded with explosive anger. She regarded it as a personal failure and was furious at being in that position. Her bitterness remained with her for a long time and made it difficult for her to work through her grief until she sought help from a grief counselor.

Guilt Shneidman has said, "I believe that the person who commits suicide puts his psychological skeletons in

the survivor's emotional closet—he sentences the survivors
to deal with many negative feelings, and more, to become
obsessed with thoughts regarding their own actual or possible role in having precipitated the suicidal act or having
failed to abort it. It can be a heavy load."[1]

That is one reason so many survivors of suicides reach
out for help from counselors and support groups. The guilt
feelings can be insidious and leave you raw. It is the self-
blame, the acceptance of the fault or responsibility for
someone's dying that is a tremendously heavy burden. You
may be questioning what you did to cause the suicide. It is
a lot of "if onlys." "If only I had been more loving and told
him more often that I loved him." "If only I had not argued
with her and said all those nasty things I did not mean." "If
only I had not broken off our relationship." If only. . .if
only. Maybe it is not what you did, but what you did not
do. Maybe you are feeling guilty because you think you
could have done something to prevent the suicide if only
you had recognized the warning signs or insisted on getting
professional help.

Guilt may become deep and haunting. Who was responsible for the death, and what was your role? It is common
for survivors to go over and over the days before the
suicide to search for reasons to relieve the guilt. If you
lived under the threat of suicide before it actually happened, you may be experiencing relief and then guilt on
top of that just for being relieved. You also may have guilt
feelings for being angry at the person who committed
suicide: You aren't supposed to be angry at someone who
is dead, so you feel guilty for being angry. Guilt has you
coming and going. It will take a tremendous amount
of effort to control the guilt feelings, deserved and unde-

[1] Cain, A.C., ed. *Survivors of Suicide*. Thomas, 1972.

served, and some residue may be there for the rest of your life. The challenge is to accept it and find atonement for it.

B. THE COURSE OF GRIEF: TASKS AND WORK

Everyone who suffers a loss and mourns a death does so in his or her own way. The expected and unexpected feelings may or may not apply to you. People who survive a suicide in their family appear to go through stages as their grief progresses from the immobilizing pain of shock, sadness, fear, anger, or guilt to a freedom that comes with healing. J. William Worden[2] describes what happens during these stages as a series of tasks. It makes sense to think of mourning in terms of tasks because grief doesn't resolve itself with time. It takes effort to allow yourself to face and accomplish each task. If you avoid them, which may be far easier at the time, the healing may not be completed. This is called blocking, or incomplete bereavement. It is much like getting a splinter in your finger: The thought of digging into the already sore spot may lead you just to clean it and wrap a bandage around it, hoping the splinter will work its way out eventually. The spot is tender and you protect it, but the wound becomes infected and you finally remove the splinter with a needle so the sore can heal properly.

WORDEN'S FOUR TASKS OF MOURNING

Task I. To accept the reality of the loss.

Immediately following the news of the death, you may shake your head in disbelief, refusing to believe it has

[2] J. William Worden. *Grief Counseling and Grief Therapy*. Springer, 1982.

really happened. There is a hope that it was a mistake, that the police have identified the wrong person, or the doctors were in error when they pronounced him dead. Getting yourself to accept the fact that your friend or loved one is dead and will not come back is the first task of grief. Denial may last only for a brief time, but a glimmer of the disbelief may linger. You may so intensely want to believe that it didn't happen that your denial leads you to see the face of the deceased in a crowd or think you hear him speaking in another room. You will need to remind yourself over and over that death has taken your loved one.

Some families find it most difficult to accept the fact that the death was a suicide. They press for an investigation into the possibility of homicide or insist that the death was accidental even to the point of hiding evidence from the authorities. The energy put into denial detracts from the effort needed to accept the reality of the loss.

Along with struggling to accept the death, you experience the shock and numbness in the first stage of grief. As it lessens, the full impact of the loss—its meaning for you and how much you will miss the person who has committed suicide—hits you full force.

Task II. To experience the pain of grief.

Television and movie dramas depict the hero or heroine grieving over a friend's death with a brief scene of holding the deceased in his arms and a camera close-up of the tears. The next scene moves on to the business of the day, whether it be solving the mystery or plotting intrigue. Perhaps we, as viewers, would be too uncomfortable seeing people mourn as they do in real ife. Perhaps the hero or heroine would no longer be sympathetic, but pathetic. We want to see stoicism so we can be proud of their strength and say to ourselves, I want to be just like them if that should happen to me.

The task at hand for someone to complete the mourning process is to allow the grief to be felt and expressed. It is okay to hurt and to let it happen. If you believe the subtle message of our society that you should not grieve, this task will be very difficult to achieve and your grief work may be blocked. Everyone faces this task in his own way. The important thing is not to suppress the pain, or the whole course of mourning will be prolonged.

A father of a teenage girl who had killed herself six weeks earlier was able to talk about his anguish. He described how he was preoccupied with thoughts of her and felt great waves of pain. He said his best friend told him it was time to move on, to forget his daughter because she was dead, and to turn his attention to his work and his other children who were living and needed him. He looked at his friend and slowly said, "I do not want to feel this way six months from now or one year from now. As much as I don't want to experience this, I know I must."

It is quite normal to be depressed during this stage of bereavement. If someone does not consciously face grief and avoids experiencing the pain following a suicidal death, the effects will be felt much later. Most often it surfaces as a serious depression needing professional help to resolve it.

You can also expect not to feel well physically during this period of mourning. The grief leaves the body exposed and vulnerable to physical ailments. It is difficult to eat when you have no appetite and difficult to sleep when you lie in bed thinking and hurting. Some people try to skip the task of experiencing the pain of grief by medicating themselves with tranquilizers, sleeping pills, and alcohol. For mourning ever to be completed, this stage cannot be skipped, and drugs only serve to prolong the inevitable.

The guilt that is felt by survivors of a suicide surfaces in this stage of mourning and may reappear for a long time. Families use the energy generated by guilt and anger to search for reasons why the deceased chose to die. Perhaps they can let go of some of the guilt if they can convince themselves that it was someone else's fault or there really was nothing they could have done to prevent the suicide. It is an endless search and there is no answer because the only person who could know is dead. Sometimes a suicide note gives clues, but most of the time there is no note. It is a sign of progress in grief work if survivors can accept the fact that there are no answers and can begin to redirect their energies to accomplishing the tasks of grief.

The sharpness of the pain will eventually turn into a dull yearning sensation. The longing may surface from time to time with memories of the deceased. As you progress through grief you can expect to experience these episodes less and less frequently. In a way, grief may never be over. Memories can trigger sadness even ten years after the loss. If this second task is completed successfully, the memories can also trigger a pleasant experience of joy and thankfulness for having had the opportunity to share your lives for as long as you did.

Task III. To adjust to an environment in which the deceased is missing.

Exactly what you need to adjust to depends on what role the suicide victim played in your life and what your relationship was. If a parent committed suicide, you may be forced to assume more responsibility for yourself and others in the family as well as seek guidance and support from someone else. If the deceased was a sibling or friend, the meaning of the loss will be different. With whom will you have lunch, talk on the phone, complain about the overload of homework, trade clothes, go to the movies, or walk to school? These may seem like small things to others, but they can leave a void for you to get used to. If you are grieving over the loss of a special boyfriend or girlfriend, it can mean giving up dreams of a future together as well as the absence of a companion and lover now.

The danger in not adjusting to your new environment without your lost loved one is conceding your own helplessness and prolonging dependency by letting others do things for you when you are ready to do things for yourself. Just like someone who works through a crisis by learning new ways to solve problems, to cope, grief work gives you an opportunity to get in touch with abilities you may not have realized you had and to learn to face these challenges with new skills.

Task IV. To withdraw emotional energy and reinvest it in another relationship.

This is the last task of grieving and in many ways the most difficult. You may think that no one could ever take the place of your lost loved one. In one sense that is true. That part of yourself is reserved for memories. The task for you now is to redirect your love to other persons and to open up to a new relationship. This is what we call putting the pieces back together. It is the relations we form that become the primary meaning in life. This is how you can grow. This is the new you.

C. RESPONDING TO THE NEEDS OF OTHERS

All of us are confronted with grief at some time in our life. Most of us have little preparation for facing it ourselves or helping someone else survive its impact. We are sheltered from mourning and bereavement as children. Adults are uncomfortable mourning in the presence of children and want to protect them from unhappiness and suffering. Children are frequently spared from attending a funeral or visiting a funeral home. Questions go unasked and unanswered. In this way well-meaning but uninformed parents may not give their children the opportunity to share the family's grief. Loss is felt deeply regardless of the desire by adults to protect children from the impact. It is very difficult for children to learn to cope with losses without this opportunity to observe and experience grief within their family.

If you have reached your teenage years without having had an opportunity to observe your parents support a bereaved friend or have friends support your family in time of mourning, you may wonder what you can say or do to be helpful to someone else who is grieving. If the death is a suicide, the role of caring, understanding friends is vital to help survivors work through their grief so they will be able to accept the loss.

People grieve differently and have different needs, but many share common problems and needs. If support from family and friends is not available or is refused, the grief work becomes much more difficult. Suicide survivors are at a higher risk for also dying by suicide. Helping someone survive a suicide may prevent an additional suicide. If you are in a position to give this support, read the following points carefully. If you are suffering the loss yourself, see if these fit for you and think how and from whom you can ask for help.

1. A need to talk about the details of the suicide

When the news of the death reaches a survivor, the emotional impact may make it difficult to absorb or understand everything that is being said. It may seem like a bad dream that will disappear upon waking. If the survivor is the one who discovered the body, the shock of the scene could block out many of the details. The scene may reappear in nightmares or many years later. Or friends may wish to withhold these details from other close survivors, thinking that it will help protect them if they are not exposed to the horrifying facts. Police and authorities must investigate each suicide and rule out the possibility of accidental death or homicide. Survivors are often questioned extensively to assist in this investigation. They may even be suspected as a murderer. Confusion and shock make it difficult to understand what has happened.

The first task challenging a suicide survivor is to accept the fact that the loved one is dead and that it was suicide. Going over the information and details time and time again is one way to accomplish this grief work. Talking about the event helps one to accept its reality. Questions are asked and an attempt is made to put the pieces together until the picture becomes complete. As a friend, you can help find out some mssing details or patiently listen to the survivor tell the story over and over. This does not imply that it is necessary to dwell on a gory scene. Ask where he was when he learned about the death. It is amazing how sharp these memories are—or sometimes how the mind becomes protective against the pain and forgets what happened altogether.

Help the survivor realize that the death was not an accident or a homicide. Shame and embarrassment may make it very difficult for him to admit that the death was self-inflicted. The old stigma is still prevalent in our society. Denying the suicide complicates the grief. Peter Fonda's mother committed suicide while she was confined to a mental institution when Peter was a young boy. He was told that she had died but not how. That fact he learned as a young adult. He described how he felt when he was finally told the truth by his sister, Jane. He felt the despair and anguish as fresh grief because the information had been withheld from him earlier, and he had to mourn her death all over again.

2. A need to search for reasons

It seems to be important for survivors to expend some energy in searching for the cause of the suicide. "Why did he do it?" "What could have been so horrible in his life that he wanted to die?"

Guilt is something that most survivors experience to some degree, and guilt generates uneasiness or even torment. If someone or something else can be blamed, or at least share the blame, it may bring some relief and ease the discomfort of the guilt. The search for understanding does not necessarily mean that the guilty feelings are the only motivation behind those efforts. They may think that answers would help them accept the death as a suicide, would provide a reason for such an "unreasonable" act and bring sense out of "nonsense." The survivors want to understand everything they can, not only about the events that led to the death, but also about what was going through the victim's mind. Books about suicide and the grief following suicide are excellent resources to offer survivors. See the Bibliography for suggestions.

Notice that this need to know why was explained as a need to search for reasons. It is the activity, the expending of energy, that is much more important than the answers themselves. In fact the answers usually are never known because they are buried with the deceased. Very few suicide victims leave a note that sufficiently explains why they are rejecting life. A survivor may interpret the suicide as a rejection or abandonment of himself. That is very difficult to accept. Survivors eventually give up the search. Once they can emotionally and intellectually accept the fact that they will never know the reasons and that they are not responsible for their loved one's death, they can use that energy to adjust to an environment is which the deceased is missing. It is a hopeful sign that they are progressing through the tasks of grief.

3. A need to express feelings

The expected and unexpected feelings that follow such a traumatic death were described earlier: sadness, anger, guilt, anxiousness, fear, shock, and shame. Sadness is the most noticeable emotion and probably lasts the longest. Guilt is the most insidious. Sometimes there may even be an element of relief if there has been a period of fear that suicide might occur or a period of turmoil and suffering. The unpleasant aspect of grief may keep survivors from either recognizing the feelings or experiencing them to the depth they need to be felt to work through the second stage of mourning. Just being there to acknowledge the feelings and impact of the loss will be greatly appreciated by a suicide survivor. Review the listening skills described in Chapter 5. Don't ask "How do you feel?" Imagine what he is feeling and give the feeling a name. Don't say that you know how he feels. You probably don't unless you are also a survivor. A comment such as, "This is a terrible experience for you, and I know you are devastated over the loss of your friend," is an example of reflecting the spoken or unspoken grief. Don't be surprised if it brings on a flow of tears. Tears are normal. A touch or hug may be comforting. Allow time for sobbing with no conversation. Crying helps, especially when you cry with good friends.

It is important not to try to take away the pain by attempting to cheer up a survivor with unnecessary distractions or unwanted activities. Refrain from encouraging him to mask the feelings with sleeping pills or medication. Remember, the pain must be felt to continue on the path toward recovery. If feelings are buried or avoided they will cause problems later. That is what professional grief counselors call being stuck or blocked. It is not unusual for a death of a loved one to bring up feelings of grief from a previous loss. You might want to ask if he is remembering other sad times. Help your friend to describe what is going on inside, accept the tears, and cry with him if you feel like it. Crying is both healthy and therapeutic but some people do not cry when they are sad. Others cry when they are angry, or even happy. It is okay to express feelings in different ways. Let him dig deep into the dark well of emotions and bring them to the light of day. It may be surprising to find anger a part of grief. The anger can even be directed toward the deceased. Sometimes people are embarrassed to express their grief in front of others, so you must let them know it is safe and okay with you. This may be gut-wrenching for you also. Be prepared to be exhausted afterward.

6. A need to know what is happening and what will happen during grief

The normal path of grief takes many turns. Your friend may be bewildered and frightened by what is going on. Sometimes a bereaved person thinks he sees or hears his missing loved one. It seems so real that he may think he is going crazy. You can reassure him that this is quite normal. It doesn't mean he is going crazy, but it does mean he misses the deceased very much and wishes the death hadn't happened. You can explain that a lot of confusing things go on during grief. It is difficult to concentrate and make decisions. Interest and productivity at work or school may be lost for a while. Sleep may not come easily, so feeling tired and listless is common. The appetite diminishes and weight loss is also common. Because the body is in such stress, a person who is grieving is very vulnerable to physical problems. Friends can help monitor a survivor's health for a while and encourage checkups from a physician.

Sometimes it is comforting to read about the grief process and what to expect during the time of mourning. A gift of a book about grief and surviving suicide would be appreciated. Knowledge can relieve the fear and anxiety. It won't make the grief go away, but it will make it a little easier.

7. A need for continuing support

How long does grief last? No matter how long, the survivor who mourns the death thinks it is too long. He longs for the day when the heart will not be so heavy, when sleep comes more easily, and the joy of life is recaptured. He does not need to hear from well-meaning friends four weeks after the suicide that it is time to put the grief aside. There are no time scales or deadlines that say mourning should be completed by such-and-such a date. Have you ever seen a cowboy movie where someone is killed and buried? Life goes on for the brave widow almost immediately as if nothing had happened. It might spoil the story if the concept of the heroine's pioneer spirit was tarnished to permit a period of mourning.

Mourning is a time for healing and a time to regain a balance. Even after a survivor is able to laugh again and get back to work or school, the inner pain may continue. Be sensitive to special anniversaries. The birthday of the deceased, a year after they first started going together, or graduation ceremonies can be a difficult time for a survivor. If holidays were spent together, the next Christmas or Thanksgiving can bring tears. You can mention how much the deceased is missed and talk about what they used to do together on this day or what plans they had for future holidays or anniversaries. Be aware that it will take survivors of suicide a long time to work through the anger and guilt in addition to the despair and anguish that come with mourning. Expect the grief after a suicide to last up to two years. There will be ups and downs along the way. A friend's continuing support and sensitivity to the continuing needs of survivors is important.

D. SUMMARY

Grief is the mental suffering that accompanies bereavement. The feelings that follow a suicide include shame, remorse, fear, anger, and guilt as well as shock, sadness, and distress. The course of bereavement is frequently described as a series of stages. It is even more helpful to view them as tasks, because grief is work and it takes effort as well as time for the feelings to be relieved. Worden lists those tasks as: (1) to accept the reality of the loss; (2) to experience the pain; (3) to adjust to an environment in which the deceased is missing; and (4) to withdraw emotional energy and reinvest it in another relationship.

Survivors of suicide have special needs. Friends can help by being aware of those needs and being a support during the period of mourning. Some of the needs are: (1) to talk about the details of the suicide; (2) to search for reasons; (3) to express feelings; (4) to be alone as well as have companionship; to have assistance as well as independence; and (5) for continuing support.

REFERENCES

John H. Hewett. *After Suicide*. Westminster Press, 1980.

Appendix

APPENDIX A

Exercise I Key for identifying feelings

Statements 2, 5, 11, 12, 18, and 19 are clearly statements that express the present feelings of the speaker.

Statement 6 indicates what the speaker *would* feel but not what he or she *is* feeling.

Statement 4 *(pushed around)*, 7 *(rejected)*, 10 *(dominated)*, and 20 *(misunderstood)* describe what someone else is *doing to* the speaker. Ask "How do you feel when someone does that to you?"

Statement 16 says what the speaker is *not* feeling instead of what he or she *is* feeling.

Statement 9 is a thought.

The other statements (1, 3, 8, 13, 14, 15, and 17) have *like* or *that* after the word *feel*, which indicate a thought.

Exercise II Stimulus Statements I

These responses most closely convey empathy—a caring, understanding, and accepting response.

1. B. I bet you feel a lot better now.

2. C. You must be disgusted.

3. B. You are pleased that I understand what it is like.

4. A. You must be relieved to be able to pay your bill.

5. D. It sounds like you are pretty desperate.

6. B. It sounds like you are proud of yourself.

7. D. You are really mad that she didn't come.

8. A. You are glad that he took so much time with you.

9. C. You are worried about her.

10. C. You are really furious at her.

11. A. You are satisfied with the test.

12. D. You feel sorry for her.

13. B. You are content with the way you reacted.

14. C. You feel sad because of what happened.

15. A. You are certainly peeved at her.

16. A. You are excited that you may get to go there.

17. C. It sounds like you are pretty bitter.

18. C. You are pleased with the team's potential.

19. B. You are delighted that he treated you with respect.

20. C. You are annoyed that you spent so much on it.

21. A. You feel lonely.

22. B. You're eager about that class.

23. D. You are enthusiastic.

Exercise III Stimulus Statements II

The following are responses that identify the feeling and the most important point in each of the paragraphs and responses that would not promote understanding.

1. *Promotes understanding*
   You feel miserable because you aren't treated with respect at school.

Doesn't promote understanding
I don't blame you for wanting to quit. If I were treated that
way I would never go back.

2. *Promotes understanding*
   You are discouraged because your dad got so mad last night.
   Doesn't promote understanding
   You should not even have told him you wanted to quit
   school.
   No sense in upsetting him and running the risk of getting
   grounded or, worse yet, giving him an excuse to hit you.

3. *Promotes understanding*
   You are really upset because he didn't understand what is
   going on with you.
   Doesn't promote understanding
   I got grounded last month for something I didn't even do. I
   really feel sorry for you.

4. *Promotes understanding*
   You feel confused because you aren't sure what your dad
   expects of you or even if he cares if you leave home.
   Doesn't promote understanding
   Maybe if you left it would get back at him for making your
   life at home so intolerable.

5. *Promotes understanding*
   You feel frustrated because your mom and dad gripe and yell
   at you.
   Doesn't promote understanding
   Why don't you yell and gripe back at them?

6. *Promotes understanding*
   You are annoyed because your mom is always on your back
   and won't leave you alone.
   Doesn't promote understanding
   My mom does that to me too.

7. *Promotes understanding*
You feel confused because you aren't happy at home or school and don't know where you do fit.
Doesn't promote understanding
Cheer up. At least you have some neat friends.

8. *Promotes understanding*
You seem so discouraged because you don't see yourself fitting in and sometimes you wish you were never born.
Doesn't promote understanding
I read a book the other day where this guy actually wished he never existed and then saw how his family lived without him. It was weird.

9. *Promotes understanding*
You are weary and frustrated because on the one hand you know your folks love you and on the other hand it's hard to believe it because of the way they treat you.
Doesn't promote understanding
It doesn't matter if they love you or not. You don't need them.

10. *Promotes understanding*
You feel helpless because you don't seem to be able to change your relationship with your parents.
Doesn't promote understanding
It never makes sense to expect parents to be reasonable.

11. *Promotes understanding*
You feel so isolated and sad because no one seems to understand.
Doesn't promote understanding
That's just something you will have to get used to.

APPENDIX B

Suicide Prevention and Crisis Intervention Hotlines in the United States

Alabama

ANDALUSIA
SOUTH CENTRAL MENTAL
HEALTH BOARD
HELPLINE
Crisis Phone:(205)222-7794
AUBURN
CRISIS CENTER OF E.
ALABAMA, INC.
Crisis Phone:(205)821-8600
BIRMINGHAM
CRISIS CENTER, INC.
Crisis Phone:(205)323-7777
DECATUR
CRISIS CALL CENTER
NORTH CENTRAL ALABAMA
MENTAL HEALTH
CENTER
Crisis Phone:(205)355-6091
GADSDEN
13TH PLACE
Crisis Phone:(205)547-9505
HUNTSVILLE
HUNTSVILLE HELPLINE
Crisis Phone:(205)539-1000
MOBILE
CONTACT MOBILE
Crisis Phone:(205)432-1222
MOBILE MENTAL HEALTH
CENTER CRISIS
INTERVENTION
SERVICES
Crisis Phone:(205)473-4423
MONTGOMERY
HELP A CRISIS
Crisis Phone:(205)279-7837
TUSCALOOSA
CRISIS LINE/TUSCALOOSA
Crisis Phone:(205)345-1600

Alaska

ANCHORAGE
ANCHORAGE COMMUNITY
MENTAL HEALTH
SERVICES, INC.
Crisis Phone:(907)563-1000
C.R.I.S.I.S. INC.
Crisis Phone:(907)276-1600

FAIRBANKS
FAIRBANKS CRISIS CLINIC
FOUNDATION
Crisis Phone:(907)452-4357
KENAI
CENTRAL PENINSULA
COUNSELING SERVICES
Crisis Phone:(907)283-7501
KETCHIKAN
GATEWAY CENTER FOR
HUMAN SERVICES
Crisis Phone:(907)225-4135
WASILLA
MAT-SU COMMUNITY
COUNSELING CENTER
Crisis Phone:(907)376-3706

Arizona

CLIFTON
GRAHAM-GREENLEE
COMMUNITY SERVICE
CENTER
Crisis Phone:(602)865-4531
MESA
SUICIDE PREVENTION
CENTER OF MARICOPA
COUNTY
Crisis Phone:(602)249-2915
PHOENIX
PHOENIX CRISIS
INTERVENTION
PROGRAM
Crisis Phone:(602)258-8011
PSYCHIATRIC CRISIS
CENTER
Crisis Phone:(602)267-5881
TERROS AGENCY
Crisis Phone 1:(602)249-6314
Crisis Phone 2:(602)249-1749
SAFFORD
GRAHAM-GREENLEE
COUNSELING CENTER,
INC.
Crisis Phone:(602)428-5711
SCOTTSDALE
INTERFAITH COUNSELING
SERVICE SUICIDE
PREVENTION CENTER
Crisis Phone:(602)249-2915

YUMA
CASA DE YUMA SUICIDE
PREVENTION HOTLINE
Crisis Phone 1:(602)782-7273
Crisis Phone 2:(602)342-3668

Arkansas

HOT SPRINGS
COMMUNITY COUNSELING
SERVICES, INC.
Crisis Phone:(501)624-'; 11
LITTLE ROCK
CRISIS CENTER OF
ARKANSAS, INC.
Crisis Phone:(501)375-5151
PINE BLUFF
CONTACT PINE BLUFF
Crisis Phone:(501)536-4226
SPRINGDALE
NORTHWEST ARKANSAS
CRISIS INTERVENTION
CENTER
Crisis Phone 1:(501)756-2337
Crisis Phone 2:(501)631-0060

California

ANAHEIM
HOTLINE HELP CENTER
Crisis Phone:(714)778-1000
BERKELEY
SUICIDE PREVENTION OF
ALAMEDA COUNTY
Crisis Phone 1:(415)849-2212
Crisis Phone 2:(415)889-1333
Crisis Phone 3:(415)794-5211
Crisis Phone 4:(415)449-5566
BURLINGAME
SUICIDE PREVENTION/CC
OF SAN MATEO COUNTY
Crisis Phone 1:(415)692-6655
Crisis Phone 2:(415)692-6662
CAPITOLA
SUICIDE PREVENTION
SERVICE OF SANTA CRUZ
COUNTY
Crisis Phone 1:(408)458-5300
Crisis Phone 2:(408)688-1818

DAVIS
  SUICIDE PREVENTION OF
    YOLO COUNTY
  Davis:(916)756-5000
  Woodland:(916)666-7778
  West Sacramento: (916)372-6565
EL CAJON
  CRISIS HOUSE
  Crisis Phone:(619)444-1194
FORT BRAGG
  CRISIS LINE CARE PROJECT
  Crisis Phone:(707)964-4357
FORT IRWIN
  ARMY COMMUNITY
    SERVICE
  Crisis Phone:(619)386-3513
FRESNO
  CONTACT FRESNO
  Crisis Phone:(209)298-2022
  HELP IN EMOTIONAL
    TROUBLE
  Crisis Phone:(209)485-1432
GARDEN GROVE
  NEW HOPE COUNSELING
    CENTER
  Crisis Phone:(714)639-4673
LAFAYETTE
  CONTACT-CARE CENTER
  Crisis Phone:(415)284-2273
  Teen-to-Teen Hotline:(415)945-
    TEEN
  Kid-phone Warmline:(415)284-
    2274
LAKEPORT
  LAKE COUNTY MENTAL
    HEALTH EMERGENCY
    SERVICE
  Crisis Phone:(707)263-0160
LOS ALAMITOS
  WEST ORANGE COUNTY
    HOTLINE
  Crisis Phone 1:(714)761-4575
  Crisis Phone 2:(213)596-5548
  Crisis Phone 3:(714)894-4242
LOS ANGELES
  LOS ANGELES SPC
  Crisis Phone:(213)381-5111
  CENTER FOR THE STUDY
    OF PSYCHOLOGICAL
    TRAUMA
  Crisis Phone:(213)855-3569
NAPA
  NORTH BAY SUICIDE
    PREVENTION, INC.
  Fairfield:(707)422-2555
  Napa:(707)255-2555
  Vallejo:(707)643-2555
  Survivors Group: (707)544-2510
  Survivors Group: (707)257-3470
NEWARK
  SECOND CHANCE, INC.

Crisis Phone:(415)792-4357
PACIFIC GROVE
  SUICIDE PREVENTION AND
    CRISIS CENTER
  Monterey Area: (408)649-8008
  Salinas Area:(408)424-1485
  San Benito County:(408)636-
    8787
PASADENA
  CONTACT PASADENA
  Crisis Phone:(818)449-4500
RANCHO CUCAMONGA
  SUICIDE AND CRISIS
    INTERVENTION SERVICE
    INC.
  Crisis Phone:(714)945-1066
REDDING
  HELP, INC.
  Crisis Phone:(916)225-5252
REDLANDS
  EAST VALLEY CHAPTER OF
    MENTAL HEALTH
    ASSOCIATION
  Crisis Phone:(714)792-8255
SACRAMENTO
  SUICIDE PREVENTION
    SERVICE OF
    SACRAMENTO
  Crisis Phone:(916)441-1135
SAN ANSELMO
  MARIN SUICIDE
    PREVENTION CENTER
  Crisis Phone 1:(415)454-4524
  Crisis Phone 2:(415)454-4544
SAN BERNARDINO
  SUICIDE AND CRISIS
    INTERVENTION SERVICE
  Crisis Phone:(714)886-4889
SAN DIEGO
  CRISIS LINE FAMILY CRISIS
    INTERVENTION CENTER
  Crisis Phone:(619)268-7777
  THE CRISIS TEAM
  Crisis Phone:(619)236-3339
  San Diego County
    Only:(800)351-0757
SAN FRANCISCO
  SAN FRANCISCO SUICIDE
    PREVENTION
  Crisis Phone 1:(415)221-1423
  Crisis Phone 2:(415)221-1424
  Crisis Phone 3:(415)221-1428
SAN JOSE
  SANTA CLARA SUICIDE &
    CRISIS
  Crisis Phone 1:(408)279-3312
  Crisis Phone 2:(408)683-2482
SAN LUIS OBISPO
  HOTLINE OF SAN LUIS
    OBISPO COUNTY, INC.
  Crisis Phone:(805)544-6163

SANTA BARBARA
  CALL-LINE
  Crisis Phone:(805)569-2255
SANTA CRUZ
  CRISIS INTERVENTION
    SERVICE
  North County:(408)425-2237
  South County:(408)722-3577
SANTA MONICA
  NEW START
  Crisis Phone:(213)828-5561
STOCKTON
  SAN JOAQUIN COUNTY
    MENTAL HEALTH
  Crisis Phone:(209)948-4484
VENTURA
  CRISIS EVALUATION UNIT
  VENTURA COUNTY
    MENTAL HEALTH
    DEPARTMENT
  Crisis Phone:(805)652-6727
WALNUT CREEK
  CONTRA COSTA CRISIS/
    SUICIDE INTERVENTION
  Crisis Phone:(415)939-3232
YUBA CITY
  SUTTER-YUBA MENTAL
    HEALTH CRISIS CLINIC
  Crisis Phone:(916)673-8255

Colorado

ARVADA
  LIFE LINE OF COLORADO,
    INC.
  Crisis Phone:(303)458-7777
  JEFFERSON CENTER FOR
    MENTAL HEALTH
  Crisis Phone:(303)425-0300
AURORA
  COMITIS CRISIS CENTER
  Crisis Phone:(303)343-9890
BOULDER
  EMERGENCY PSYCHIATRIC
    SERVICES
  Crisis Phone:(303)447-1665
COLORADO SPRINGS
  CRISIS EMERGENCY
    SERVICES PIKES PEAK
    MENTAL HEALTH
    CENTER, INC.
  Crisis Phone:(303)471-8300
  TERROS
  Crisis Phone:(303)471-4127
DENVER
  SUICIDE AND CRISIS
    CONTROL
  Crisis Phone 1:(303)757-0988
  Crisis Phone 2:(303)789-3073
FORT MORGAN

FORT MORGAN HELPLINE
Crisis Phone 1:(303)867-3411
Crisis Phone 2:(303)867-2451
GRAND JUNCTION
CRISIS LINE
Crisis Phone:(303)242-help
PUEBLO
PUEBLO SUICIDE
PREVENTION CENTER,
INC.
Crisis Phone:(303)544-1133

Connecticut

GREENWICH
HOTLINE INC.
Greenwich Area: (203)661-
HELP
Stamford Area: (203)353-HELP
HARTFORD
INFOLINE
Crisis Phone:(203)522-4636
NORWALK
INFO LINE OF
SOUTHWESTERN
CONNECTICUT
Bridgeport:(203)333-7555
Norwalk:(203)853-2525
Stamford:(203)324-1010
PLAINVILLE
THE WHEELER CLINIC,
INC.
Crisis Phone 1:(203)747-3434
Crisis Phone 2:(203)524-1182
TRUMBULL
TRUMBULL COUNSELING
CENTER
Crisis Phone:(203)261-5110
WESTPORT
OPEN LINE, LTD.
Crisis Phone:(203)226-3546

Delaware

DOVER
KENT/SUSSEX MOBILE
CRISIS UNIT KENT/
SUSSEX COMMUNITY
MENTAL HEALTH
CENTER
In Delaware:(800)345-6785
GEORGETOWN
GEORGETOWN HELPLINE
SUSSEX COUNTY
COMMUNITY MENTAL
HEALTH CENTER
Crisis Phone:(302)856-6626
NEW CASTLE

GRTR WILMINGTON-NEW
CASTLE COUNTY
PSYCHIATRIC
EMERGENCY SERVICE
Crisis Phone 1:(302)421-6711
Crisis Phone 2:(302)421-6712
Crisis Phone 3:(302)421-6713
WILMINGTON
CONTACT-DELAWARE, INC.
Crisis Phone:(302)575-1112

Dist. of Columbia

WASHINGTON
ANDROMEDA TRANSCUL
TURAL MENTAL HEALTH
CENTER
Crisis Phone:(202)667-6766
D.C. EMERGENCY
PSYCHIATRIC RESPONSE
DIVISION
Crisis Phone:(202)561-7000
D.C. HOTLINE
Crisis Phone:(202)223-2255
FACT (FAMILIES &
CHILDREN IN TROUBLE/
TOGETHER) HOTLINE
Crisis Phone:(202)628-3228
THE SAMARITANS OF
WASHINGTON, INC.
Crisis Phone 1:(202)362-8100
Crisis Phone 2:(202)362-8661
Crisis Phone 3:(202)362-8665

Florida

BRADENTON
MANATEE GLENS
CORPORATION CRISIS
SERVICES
Crisis Phone:(813)748-8585
DE FUNIAK SPRINGS
C.O.P.E. CENTER
CHAUTAUQUA OFFICE OF
PSYCHOTHERAPY
Crisis Phone:(904)892-4357
FORT LAUDERDALE
CRISIS LINE/INFORMATION
AND REFERRAL OF
COMMUNITY SERVICE
COUNCIL OF BROWARD
COUNTY
Crisis Phone:(305)467-6333
FORT MYERS
LEE MENTAL HEALTH
CENTER, INC.
Hotline:(813)275-4242
FORT PIERCE

INDIAN RIVER COMMUNITY
MENTAL HEALTH
CENTER
Crisis Phone:(305)464-8111
FORT WALTON BEACH
CRISIS LINE/FORT WALTON
BEACH
Crisis Phone:(904)244-9191
Crestview, Toll- Free:(904)682-
0101
GAINESVILLE
ALACHUA COUNTY CRISIS
CENTER
Crisis Phone 1:(904)376-4444
Crisis Phone 2:(904)376-4445
HIALEAH
NORTHWEST DADE
COMMUNITY MENTAL
HEALTH CENTER
Crisis Phone:(305)825-0300
JACKSONVILLE
SUICIDE PREVENTION
SERVICE
Crisis Phone:(904)384-5641
KEY WEST
HELPLINE, INC. P.O. BOX
2186
Crisis Phone 1: (305)296-Help
Crisis Phone 2:(305)294-line
Middle and Upper
Keys:(800)341-4343
KISSIMMEE
HELP NOW IN OSCEOLA,
INC.
Crisis Phone:(305)847-8811
LAKE CITY
COLUMBIA COUNSELING
CENTER
Crisis Phone:(904)752-1045
After 5:00 P.M.:(904)752-2140
MIAMI
SWITCHBOARD OF MIAMI,
INC.
Crisis Phone:(305)358-4357
MILTON
AVALON CENTER CRISIS
LINE
Crisis Phone:(904)623-6363
NAPLES
HOT LINE
Crisis Phone:(813)262-7227
ORLANDO
WE CARE, INC.
Crisis Phone:(305)628-1227
Teen/Kid:(305)644-2027
MENTAL HEALTH
SERVICES OF ORANGE
Crisis Phone:(305)896-9306
PANAMA CITY
PANAMA CITY CRISIS LINE
NORTHWEST MENTAL

HEALTH CENTER
Crisis Phone:(904)769-9481
PENSACOLA
PENSACOLA HELP LINE
LAKEVIEW CENTER, INC.
Crisis Phone:(904)438-1617
PINELLAS PARK
PINELLAS EMERGENCY
MENTAL HEALTH
SERVICE, INC.
Crisis Phone 1:(813)791-3131
Crisis Phone 2:(813)791-1117
ROCKLEDGE
SUICIDE/CRISIS HOTLINE
CRISIS SERVICES OF
BREVARD, INC.
Crisis Phone:(305)631-8944
CIRCLES OF CARE, INC.
Crisis Phone:(407)723-3910
ST. PETERSBURG
HOTLINE/INFORMATION
AND REFERRAL
ALTERNATIVE HUMAN
SERVICES, INC.
Crisis Phone 1:(813)531-4664
Crisis Phone 2:(813)848-5555
Crisis Phone 3:(904)567-1111
Crisis Phone 4:(813)228-8686
SARASOTA
SUNCOAST CRISIS UNIT
Life Line:(813)955-8702
Unit Line:(813)955-9913
TALLAHASSEE
TELEPHONE COUNSELING
AND REFERRAL SERVICE
Crisis Phone:(904)224-6333
TAMPA
TAMPA HELP LINE
Crisis Phone:(813)251-4000
HILLSBOROUGH COUNTY
CRISIS CENTER
Crisis Phone:(813)238-8821
WEST PALM BEACH
CRISIS LINE INFORMATION
& REFERRAL SERVICES,
INC.
North and Central:(305)967-1000
South:(305)243-1000
West (Glades):(305)996-1121
WINTER HAVEN
HELP AND RESOURCELINE
Crisis Phone:(813)299-5858

Georgia

ATLANTA
EMERGENCY MENTAL
HEALTH SERVICE
FULTON COUNTY HEALTH

DEPARTMENT
Crisis Phone:(404)522-9222
DE KALB EMERGENCY/
CRISIS INTERVENTION
SERVICE GEORGIA
MENTAL HEALTH
INSTITUTE
Crisis Phone:(404)892-4646
AUGUSTA
HELP LINE
Crisis Phone:(404)724-4357
AUSTELL
EMERGENCY SERVICES
COBB/DOUGLAS
COMMUNITY MENTAL
HEALTH SERVICE AREA
Crisis Phone:(404)422-0202
COLUMBUS
CONTACT
CHATTAHOOCHEE
VALLEY
Crisis Phone:(404)327-3999
GAINESVILLE
CONTACT HALL COUNTY
Crisis Phone:(404)534-0617
LAWRENCEVILLE
GWINNETT/ROCKALE/
NEWTON MENTAL
HEALTH
Crisis Phone:(404)963-8141
Evening, Week-ends:(404) 963-
3223
MACON
CRISIS LINE OF MACON
AND BIBB COUNTY
MERCER UNIVERSITY
Crisis Phone:(912)745-9292
MARIETTA
COBB-DOUGLAS MENTAL
HEALTH
Crisis Phone:(404)422-0202
RIVERDALE
CLAYTON CRISIS LINE
CLAYTON GENERAL
HOSPITAL
Crisis Phone:(404)996-4357
SAVANNAH
FIRST CALL FOR HELP
Crisis Phone:(912)232-3383

Hawaii

HONOLULU
SUICIDE AND CRISIS
CENTER
Crisis Phone:(808)521-4555
KAILUA-KONA
KONA CRISIS CENTER, INC.
Crisis Phone:(808)329-9111

Idaho

BOISE
EMERGENCY LINE
REGION IV SERVICES/
MENTAL HEALTH
Crisis Phone:(208)338-7044
COEUR D' ALENE
REGION I MENTAL HEALTH
Crisis Phone:(208)667-6406
IDAHO FALLS
IDAHO FALLS EMERGENCY
SERVICES REGION VII
MENTAL HEALTH
Crisis Phone:(208)525-7129
KELLOGG
KELLOGG EMERGENCY
LINE HEALTH AND
WELFARE SERVICE
CENTER
Crisis Phone 1:(208)667-6406
Crisis Phone 2:(208)786-2781
LEWISTON
YWCA CRISIS SERVICES
Crisis Phone:(208)746-9655
ST. MARIES
ST. MARIES EMERGENCY
LINE
HEALTH AND WELFARE
SERVICE CENTER
Crisis Phone:(208)245-2527
TWIN FALLS
TWIN FALLS EMERGENCY
SERVICES REGION 5
MENTAL HEALTH
Crisis Phone:(208)734-4000

Illinois

ALTON
MADISON COUNTY
MENTAL HEALTH
CENTER
Crisis Phone:(618)463-1058
ANNA
UNION COUNTY
COUNSELING SERVICE
Crisis Phone:(618)833-8551
AURORA
CRISIS LINE OF THE FOX
VALLEY ASSOCIATION
FOR INDIVIDUAL
DEVELOPMENT
Crisis Phone:(312)897-5522
BEARDSTOWN
CASS COUNTY MENTAL
HEALTH CENTER
Crisis Phone:(217)323-2980
BLOOMINGTON
EMERGENCY CRISIS

INTERVENTION TEAM
MC LEAN COUNTY CENTER
FOR HUMAN SERVICE
Crisis Phone:(309)827-4005
PATH (PERSONAL
ASSISTANCE TELEPHONE
HELP)
Crisis Phone:(309)827-4005
Toll-Free Number: (800)322-
5015
CAIRO
CAIRO CRISIS LINE
MENTAL HEALTH CENTER
Crisis Phone:(618)734-2665
CHAMPAIGN
CHAMPAIGN COUNTY
MENTAL HEALTH
CENTER CRISIS LINE
Crisis Phone 1:(217)398-8080
Crisis Phone 2:(217)359-4141
CHICAGO
IN-TOUCH HOTLINE
STUDENT COUNSELING
SERVICE UNIVERSITY OF
ILLINOIS AT CHICAGO
Crisis Phone:(312)996-5535
CLINTON
DEWITT COUNTY HUMAN
RESOURCE CENTER
Crisis Phone:(217)935-9496
COLLINSVILLE
COMMUNITY COUNSELING
SERVICES
Crisis Phone:(618)877-4420
DANVILLE
CONTACT DANVILLE
Crisis Phone:(217)443-2273
DU QUOIN
PERRY COUNTY HELP LINE
Crisis Phone:(618)542-4357
EDGEMONT
CALL FOR HELP
SUICIDE AND CRISIS
INTERVENTION SERVICE
Crisis Phone:(618)397-0963
EDWARDSVILLE
EDWARDSVILLE
COMMUNITY
COUNSELING SERVICE
Crisis Phone:(618)877-4420
ELGIN
COMMUNITY CRISIS
CENTER
Crisis Phone:(312)697-2380
ELK GROVE
TALK LINE/KIDS LINE, INC.
Talk Line:(312)228-6400
Kids Line:(312)228-KIDS
Teen Line:(312)228-TEEN
EVANSTON
EVANSTON HOSPITAL

CRISIS INTERVENTION
Crisis Phone:(312)492-6500
FREEPORT
CONTACT STEPHENSON
COUNTY
Crisis Phone:(815)233-4357
GALESBURG
SPOON RIVER CENTER
Crisis Phone:(800)322-7143
GRANITE CITY
MENTAL HEALTH CENTER
Crisis Phone:(618)877-4420
HIGHLAND
HIGHLAND COMMUNITY
COUNSELING SERVICES
Crisis Phone:(618)877-4420
HILLSBORO
MONTGOMERY COUNTY
HELPLINE
MONTGOMERY COUNTY
COUNSELING CENTER
Crisis Phone 1:(217)532-9581
Crisis Phone 2:(217)324-5052
HOFFMAN ESTATES
INSTITUTE FOR STRESS
MANAGEMENT
Crisis Phone:(312)519-0110
JOLIET
CRISIS LINE OF WILL
COUNTY
Joliet:(815)722-3344
Frankfort:(815)469-6166
Bolingbrook:(312)759-4555
Peotone:(312)258-3333
Wilmington:(815)476-6969
WILL COUNTY MENTAL
HEALTH CENTER
Crisis Phone:(815)727-8512
LIBERTYVILLE
CONNECTION TELEPHONE
CRISIS INTERVENTION
AND REFERRAL SERVICE
Crisis Phone:(312)367-1080
LINCOLN
LINCOLN CRISIS CLINIC
LOGAN-MASON MENTAL
HEALTH
Crisis Phone:(217)732-3600
MT. VERNON
MT. VERNON CRISIS LINE
Crisis Phone:(618)242-1512
PARIS
HUMAN RESOURCES
CENTER
Days:(217)465-4118
Evenings, Weekends:(217)465-
4141
PEORIA
PEORIA CALL FOR HELP
Crisis Phone:(309)673-7373
QUINCY

QUINCY SUICIDE
PREVENTION AND CRISIS
SERVICE
Crisis Phone:(217)222-1166
ROCKFORD
CONTACT OF ROCKFORD
Crisis Phone:(815)964-4044
SULLIVAN
SULLIVAN CRISIS LINE
MOULTREE COUNTY
COUNSELING CENTER
Crisis Phone:(217)728-7611
TAYLORVILLE
TAYLORVILLE HELPLINE
CHRISTIAN COUNTY
MENTAL HEALTH
CENTER
Days:(217)824-4905
Evenings, Weekends:(217)824-
3335
WOOD RIVER
CRISIS SERVICES OF
MADISON COUNTY
Crisis Phone 1:(618)877-4420
Crisis Phone 2:(618)463-1058

Indiana

ANDERSON
CONTACT/HELP
Crisis Phone:(317)649-5211
EVANSVILLE
SOUTHWESTERN INDIANA
MENTAL HEALTH
CENTER INC.
Crisis Phone:(812)423-7791
FORT WAYNE
SWITCHBOARD, INC.
Crisis Phone:(219)456-4561
GARY
CRISIS CENTER-RAP LINE
Rap Line:(219)938-0900
GREENCASTLE
CONTACT PUTNAM COUNTY
Crisis Phone:(317)653-2645
INDIANAPOLIS
CRISIS AND SUICIDE
INTERVENTION SERVICE
Crisis Phone:(317)632-7575
LAFAYETTE
LAFAYETTE CRISIS CENTER
Crisis Phone:(317)742-0244
LAWRENCEBURG
LAWRENCEBURG CRISIS
LINE COMMUNITY
MENTAL HEALTH
CENTER
Crisis Phone:(812)537-1302
Toll-free Number: (800)832-5378
LEBANON

PROJECT HELP CRISIS
INTERVENTION SERVICE
ST. PETER'S EPISCOPAL
CHURCH
Crisis Phone:(317)482-1599
MARYVILLE
CONTACT TELEPHONE OF
BLOUNT COUNTY
Crisis Phone:(615)984-7689
MERRILLVILLE
CONTACT—CARES OF
NORTHWEST INDIANA
Crisis Phone 1:(219)769-3141
Crisis Phone 2:(219)374-7660
Crisis Phone 3:(219)462-9880
Crisis Phone 4:(219)769-3278
MONTICELLO
TWIN LAKES CONTACT—
HELP
Crisis Phone:(219)583-4357

Iowa

AMES
OPEN LINE
Crisis Phone:(515)292-7000
CEDAR RAPIDS
FOUNDATION II, INC.
Crisis Phone:(319)362-2174
In Iowa:(800)332-4224
DAVENPORT
VERA FRENCH
COMMUNITY HEALTH
CENTER SUICIDE LINE
AT MERCY HOSPITAL
Crisis Phone:(319)383-1900
DES MOINES
COMMUNITY TELEPHONE
SERVICES CRISIS LINE
SERVICE OF THE
AMERICAN RED CROSS
Crisis:(515)244-1000
Counseling:(515)244-1010
FIRST CALL FOR HELP/DES
MOINES
WATS in Iowa:(800)532-1194
DUBUQUE
PHONE A FRIEND CRISIS
LINE
Crisis Phone:(319)588-4016
IOWA CITY
IOWA CITY CRISIS
INTERVENTION CENTER
Crisis Phone:(319)351-0140
SIOUX CITY
AID CENTER
Crisis Phone:(712)252-5000
WATERLOO
CRISIS SERVICES/
WATERLOO

Crisis Phone:(319)233-8484
WEST CLEAR LAKE
SUICIDE HELP CENTER OF
IOWA
IA, IL, NE, ND, SD,
WI:(800)638-4357

Kansas

EMPORIA
EMPORIA EMERGENCY
SERVICES MENTAL
HEALTH CENTER OF E.
CENTRAL KANSAS
Crisis Phone:(316)343-2626
FORT SCOTT
FORT SCOTT HELPLINE
MENTAL HEALTH
ASSOCIATION
Crisis Phone:(316)223-2420
GARDEN CITY
GARDEN CITY AREA
MENTAL HEALTH
CENTER
Crisis Phone:(316)276-7689
HUMBOLDT
SOUTHEAST KANSAS
MENTAL HEALTH
SERVICE EMERGENCY
LINE
Crisis Phone:(316)473-2241
KANSAS CITY
WYANDOTTE MENTAL
HEALTH CENTER
WYANDOTTE COUNTY
CRISIS LINE
Crisis Phone:(913)831-1773
LAWRENCE
HEADQUARTERS, INC.
Crisis Phone:(913)841-2345
MANHATTAN
REGIONAL CRISIS CENTER
Crisis Phone:(913)539-2785
SALINA
HOTLINE CRISIS
INFORMATION AND
REFERRAL
Crisis Phone:(913)827-4747
SCOTT CITY
AREA MENTAL HEALTH
CENTER
Crisis Phone:(316)872-5338
ULYSSES
ULYSSES AREA MENTAL
HEALTH CENTER
Crisis Phone 1:(316)356-3198
Crisis Phone 2:(316)356-1226
WICHITA
SEDGWICK COUNTY
DEPARTMENT OF

MENTAL HEALTH
Crisis Phone:(316)686-7465

Kentucky

ASHLAND
PATHWAYS, INC. OF
ASHLAND CRISIS
SERVICE
Crisis Phone 1:(606)324-1141
Crisis Phone 2:(800)562-8909
BOWLING GREEN
BOWLING GREEN
HELPLINE BARREN
RIVER MENTAL HEALTH
Crisis Phone:(502)842-5642
CORBIN
CORBIN EMERGENCY
SERVICES
CUMBERLAND RIVER
COMPREHENSIVE CARE
CENTER
Crisis Phone:(606)528-7010
ELIZABETH
ELIZABETHTOWN CRISIS
LINE NORTH CENTRAL
COMPREHENSIVE CARE
CENTER
Crisis Phone:(502)769-1304
HOPKINSVILLE
HOPKINSVILLE CRISIS
LINE PENNYROYAL
REGIONAL MENTAL
HEALTH
Crisis Phone:(502)886-5163
JACKSON
HAZARD/JACKSON CRISIS
LINE
KENTUCKY RIVER
COMMUNITY CARE
Toll-free Number: (800)262-7491
LEXINGTON
COMPREHENSIVE CARE
CENTER CRISIS
INTERVENTION MENTAL
HEALTH
BLUEGRASS REGIONAL
MENTAL HEALTH
Crisis Phone:(606)233-0444
LOUISVILLE
CRISIS AND INFORMATION
CENTER SEVEN
COUNTIES SERVICES,
INC.
Crisis Phone:(502)589-4313
KY WATS:(800)221-0446
MAYSVILLE
MAYSVILLE CRISIS LINE
COMPREHEND, INC.
DISTRICT MENTAL

HEALTH
Crisis Phone:(606)564-4016
MOREHEAD
PATHWAYS, INC. OF
MOREHEAD
Crisis Phone:(800)562-8909
OWENSBORO
GREEN RIVER
COMPREHENSIVE CARE
CENTER CRISIS LINE
Crisis Phone:(502)684-9466
PADUCAH
PADUCAH CRISIS LINE
WESTERN KENTUCKY
REGIONAL MENTAL
HEALTH
Crisis Phone:(800)592-3980
PRESTONSBURG
PRESTONSBURG HELPLINE
MOUNTAIN
COMPREHENSIVE CARE
CENTER
Crisis Phone:(800)422-1060

Louisiana

ALEXANDRIA
FIRST CALL FOR HELP/
ALEXANDRIA
Crisis Phone:(318)443-2255
BATON ROUGE
BATON ROUGE CRISIS
INTERVENTION CENTER
Crisis Phone:(504)924-3900
DE RIDDER
BEAUREGARD DE RIDDER
COMMUNITY HELP-LINE
Crisis Phone:(318)462-0609
HOUMA
HOUMA-TERREBONNE
CRISIS LINE
Crisis Phone:(504)872-1111
LAFAYETTE
CYPRESS HOSPITAL
Crisis Phone 1: (318)251-LIVE
Crisis Phone 2: (800)522-LYCL
SOUTHWEST LOUISIANA
EDUCATION AND
REFERRAL CENTER
Crisis Phone: (318)232-HELP
MONROE
MAIN LINE
Crisis Phone:(318)387-5683
NEW ORLEANS
RIVER OAKS CRISIS CENTER
Crisis Phone:(504)733-2273
UNITED WAY CRISIS LINE
PROGRAM
Crisis Phone:(504)523-2673

OPELOUSAS
ST. LANDRY PARISH
SUICIDE PREVENTION
PROGRAM
Crisis Phone:(318)942-4673
SLIDELL
SLIDELL CRISIS LINE, INC.
Crisis Phone:(504)643-6832
VILLE PLATTE
VILLE PLATTE M.H.C.I.C.
Crisis Phone:(318)363-5579

Maine

BANGOR
DIAL HELP
Crisis Phone:(207)947-6143
Toll-free Number: (800)431-7810
LEWISTON
TRI COUNTY MENTAL
HEALTH SERVICES
CRISIS INTERVENTION
UNIT
Crisis Phone:(207)783-4680
PORTLAND
INGRAHAM VOLUNTEERS,
INC.
Crisis Phone: (207)774-HELP
SKOWHEGAN
CRISIS STABILIZATION
UNIT
Augusta:(207)626-3448
Skowhegan:(800)452-1933

Maryland

BALTIMORE
BALTIMORE CRISIS
CENTER
WALTER P. CARTER
MENTAL HEALTH
CENTER
Crisis Phone:(301)528-2200
BALTIMORE CRISIS LINE
Weekdays:(301)578-5457
Evenings and
Weekends:(301)578-5000
FIRST STEP YOUTH
SERVICES CENTER
Crisis Phone:(301)521-3800
BOWIE
BOWIE HOTLINE
Crisis Phone:(301)262-2433
COLUMBIA
GRASS ROOTS
Crisis Phone:(301)531-6677
KENSINGTON

MONTGOMERY COUNTY
HOTLINE
Crisis Phone:(301)949-6603
RIVERDALE
PRINCE GEORGE'S COUNTY
HOTLINE AND SUICIDE
PREVENTION CENTER
Crisis Phone 1:(301)577-4866
Crisis Phone 2:(301)731-0004
SALISBURY
LIFE CRISIS CENTER, INC.
Crisis Phone: (301)749-HELP
WALDORF
COMMUNITY CRISIS AND
REFERRAL CENTER
Crisis Phone 1:(301)645-3336
Crisis Phone 2:(301)843-1110
Crisis Phone 3:(301)645-3337

Massachusetts

ACTON
CODE HOTLINE
Crisis Phone 1:(508)263-8777
Crisis Phone 2:(508)486-3130
AMESBURY
NORTH ESSEX HEALTH
RESOURCE CENTER
Crisis Phone:(800)892-0818
ATTLEBORO
NEW HOPE/ATTLEBORO
Crisis Phone 1:(508)695-2113
Crisis Phone 2:(508)762-1530
Crisis Phone 3:(508)824-4757
BEVERLY
PROJECT RAP, INC.
Crisis Phone:(617)922-0000
BOSTON
THE SAMARITANS
Crisis Phone:(617)247-0220
Samariteen Line: (617)247-8050
FALL RIVER
SAMARITANS OF FALL
RIVER–NEW BEDFORD
Crisis Phone:(617)636-6111
FALMOUTH
SAMARITANS ON CAPE COD
Crisis Phone 1:(617)548-8900
Crisis Phone 2:(617)548-8901
FRAMINGHAM
SAMARITANS OF SOUTH
MIDDLESEX, INC.
Crisis Phone 1:(617)875-4500
Crisis Phone 2:(617)478-7877
GREENFIELD
GREENFIELD EMERGENCY✳
SERVICES
9A-5P, M-F:(413)774-2758
After Hours:(800)322-0424

HOPEDALE
COMMUNITY COUNSELING
CENTER OF BLACKSTONE
VALLEY
Crisis Phone:(617)473-6723
LAWRENCE
SAMARITANS OF THE
MERRIMACK VALLEY
Crisis Phone 1:(508)688-6607
Crisis Phone 2:(508)452-6733
Crisis Phone 3:(508)372-7200
Crisis Phone 4:(508)462-6100
NEW BEDFORD
NEW BEDFORD CRISIS
CENTER
Crisis Phone:(617)996-3154
NEWBURYPORT
TURNING POINT HOT LINE
Crisis Phone:(617)465-8800
NEWTONVILLE
CONTACT BOSTON
Crisis Phone:(617)244-4350
NORTH ADAMS
HELP LINE, INC.
Crisis Phone:(413)663-6555
NORTHAMPTON
NORTHAMPTON
EMERGENCY SERVICES
Crisis Phone:(413)586-5555
NORWOOD
PULSE HOTLINE
Crisis Phone:(617)762-5144
SOUTH NORFOLK
SCREENING AND
EMERGENCY TEAM
Crisis Phone:(607)769-8670
SOUTHBRIDGE
TRI-LINK, INC
Crisis Phone:(617)765-9101
STONEHEN
EASTERN MIDDLESEX
CRISIS INTERVENTION
Crisis Phone:(617)662-6623
WARE
WARE HELPLINE VALLEY
HUMAN SERVICES
Crisis Phone:(413)283-3473
WORCESTER
CRISIS CENTER, INC.
Crisis Phone:(617)791-6562

Michigan

ADRIAN
CALL SOMEONE
CONCERNED
Crisis Phone:(517)263-6737
Toll-free Number: (800)322-0044
ANN ARBOR

WASHTENAW COUNTY
COMMUNITY MENTAL
HEALTH CENTER
Crisis Phone:(313)996-4747
BIRMINGHAM
COMMON GROUND
Crisis Phone:(313)645-9676
CENTREVILLE
ST. JOSEPH COUNTY
COMMUNITY MENTAL
HEALTH
Crisis Phone 1:(800)622-3967
Crisis Phone 2:(616)467-6351
Crisis Phone 3:(616)467-6331
DETROIT
CONTACT LIFE LINE
Crisis Phone:(313)894-5555
NSO EMERGENCY
TELEPHONE SERVICE
SUICIDE PREVENTION
CENTER
Crisis Phone:(313)224-7000
EAST LANSING
LISTENING EAR OF EAST
LANSING
Crisis Phone:(517)337-1717
FLINT
FLINT EMERGENCY
SERVICE GENESEE
COUNTY MENTAL
HEALTH
Crisis Phone:(313)257-3740
GRAND HAVEN
GRAND HAVEN HELPLINE
OTTAWA COUNTY
MENTAL HEALTH
CENTER
Crisis Phone:(616)842-4357
HART
OCEANA COUNTY
COMMUNITY MENTAL
HEALTH
Crisis Phone:(616)873-2108
HOLLAND
HOLLAND HELPLINE
Crisis Phone:(616)396-4357
Grand Haven:(616)842-4357
Grand Rapids:(616)458-4357
JACKSON
AWARE, INC.—HELPLINE
Crisis Phone:(517)783-2671
KALAMAZOO
GRYPHON PLACE
Crisis Phone:(616)381-4357
LAPEER
LAPEER COUNTY
COMMUNITY MENTAL
HEALTH CENTER
Crisis Phone:(313)667-0500
LIVONIA
TELEPHONE LISTENING

CENTER
Crisis Phone:(313)422-4852
MT. CLEMENS
MACOMB COUNTY CRISIS
CENTER
Crisis Phone:(313)573-8700
MT. PLEASANT
LISTENING EAR CRISIS
CENTER, INC.
Crisis Phone:(517)772-2918
MUSKEGON
COMMUNITY MENTAL
HEALTH SERVICES OF
MUSKEGON COUNTY
Crisis Phone:(616)722-4357
NORTHVILLE
PSYCHOTHERAPY AND
COUNSELING SERVICES
Crisis Phone: (313)348-1100
PLYMOUTH
TURNING POINT CRISIS
CENTER
Crisis Phone:(313)455-4900
PORT HURON
BLUE WATER MENTAL
HEALTH AND CHILD
GUIDANCE CLINIC
Crisis Phone:(313)985-5125
After Hours:(313)985-7161
Crisis Phone 3:(800)462-6350
CENTER FOR HUMAN
RESOURCES
Crisis Phone 1:(313)985-7161
Free in 313 Area:(800)462- 6350
ST. CLAIR COUNTY
COMMUNITY MENTAL
HEALTH SERVICES
Crisis Phone:(313)985-7161
ROYAL OAK
THE SANCTUARY
Crisis Phone:(313)547-2260
ST. JOSEPH
ST. JOSEPH HELPLINE
RIVERWOOD COMMUNITY
MENTAL HEALTH
CENTER
Crisis Phone:(616)927-4447
Toll-free Number: (800)422-0757
THE LINK CRISIS
INTERVENTION CENTER
Crisis Phone:(616)983-6351
TRAVERSE CITY
THIRD LEVEL CRISIS
INTERVENTION CENTER
INC.
Crisis Phone:(616)922-4800
In-state Toll-free: (800)442-7315
Crisis Phone 3:(616)922-4801
YPSILANTI
SOS CRISIS CENTER
Crisis Phone:(313)485-3222

Minnesota

ALEXANDRIA
 LISTENING EAR CRISIS
  CENTER
 Crisis Phone:(612)763-6638
AUSTIN
 VICTIMS CRISIS CENTER
 Crisis Phone:(507)437-6680
BRAINERD
 CROW WING COUNTY
  CRISIS AND REFERRAL
  SERVICE
 Crisis and Referral: (612)828-
  HELP
GRAND RAPIDS
 FIRST CALL FOR HELP/
  ITASCA COUNTY
 Crisis Phone:(218)326-8565
MINNEAPOLIS
 CONTACT TWIN CITIES
 Crisis Phone:(612)341-2896
 CRISIS INTERVENTION
  CENTER
 Crisis:(612)347-3161
 Suicide:(612)347-2222
 Crisis Home Program:(612)347-
  3170
 YES-NEON
 Crisis Phone:(612)379-6363
OWATONNA
 OWATONNA—STEELE
  COUNTY CONTACT
 Crisis Phone:(507)451-9100
ST. PAUL
 1ST CALL FOR HELP
 Crisis Phone:(612)291-4666

Mississippi

HATTIESBURG
 HATTIESBURG HELP LINE,
  INC.
 Crisis Phone: (601)544-HELP
JACKSON
 CONTACT JACKSON
 Crisis Phone:(601)969-2077
MERIDIAN
 WEEMS MENTAL HEALTH
  CENTER
 Crisis Phone:(601)483-4821

Missouri

CAPE GIRARDEAU
 COMMUNITY COUNSELING
  CENTER
 Crisis Phone:(800)356-5395

JOPLIN
 JOPLIN CRISIS
  INTERVENTION, INC.
 Crisis Phone:(417)781-2255
KANSAS CITY
 K.C. SUICIDE PREVENTION
  LINE
 WESTERN MISSOURI
  MENTAL HEALTH
  CENTER
 Crisis Phone 1:(816)471-3939
 Crisis Phone 2:(816)471-3940
KIRKSVILLE
 LAUGHLIN PAVILION
 In-state:(800)223-5171
 Out-of-state:(800)223-5170
NEVADA
 HSA HEARTLAND
  HOSPITAL
 Crisis Phone:(800)492-2139
ST. JOSEPH
 CRISIS INTERVENTION/ST.
  JOSEPH
 Crisis Phone:(816)232-1655
ST. LOUIS
 CONTACT ST. LOUIS
 Crisis Phone:(314)771-0404
 LIFE CRISIS SERVICES, INC
 Crisis Phone:(314)647-4357

Montana

BILLINGS
 BILLINGS HELPLINE
 YELLOWSTONE COUNTY
  WELFARE
 Crisis Phone:(406)248-1691
 HELPLINE—MENTAL
  HEALTH CENTER
 Crisis Phone:(406)252-1212
BOZEMAN
 BOZEMAN HELP CENTER
 Crisis Phone:(406)248-1691
GREAT FALLS
 COMMUNITY HELP LINE
  OF GREAT FALLS
 Crisis Phone:(406)453-4357
HELENA
 MENTAL HEALTH
  SERVICES, INC./HELENA
 Crisis Phone:(406)442-0640

Nebraska

LINCOLN
 CONTACT, INC.
 Crisis Phone:(402)464-0602
 PERSONAL CRISIS SERVICE

 Crisis Phone:(402)475-5171
NORFOLK
 24 HOUR HOTLINE
 NORTHERN NEBRASKA
  COMPREHENSIVE
  MENTAL HEALTH
  CENTER
 Crisis Phone:(800)672-8323
NORTH PLATTE
 RICHARD YOUNG FAMILY
  LIFE CENTER
 Crisis Phone:(308)532-9332
OMAHA
 THE CRISIS LINE, INC.
 Crisis Phone 1:(402)341-9111
 Crisis Phone 2:(402)341-9112

Nevada

LAS VEGAS
 SUICIDE PREVENTION
  CENTER OF CLARK
  COUNTY
 Crisis Phone:(702)731-2990
RENO
 SUICIDE PREVENTION AND
  CRISIS CALL CENTER
 Crisis Phone:(702)323-6111

New Hampshire

BERLIN
 BERLIN EMERGENCY
  SERVICES
 ANDROSCOGGIN VALLEY
  MENTAL HEALTH CLINIC
 Crisis Phone:(603)752-7404
CONCORD
 EMERGENCY SERVICES/
  CONCORD
 Crisis Phone:(603)228-1551
 HELP LINE/MERRIMACK
  COUNTY
 COMMUNITY SERVICE
  COUNCIL OF
  MERRIMACK COUNTY
 Crisis Phone 1:(603)225-4033
 Crisis Phone 2:(603)225-9000
DOVER
 STRAFFORD GUIDANCE
  CENTER, INC.
 EMERGENCY CRISIS TEAM
 Crisis Phone 1:(603)742-0630
 Crisis Phone 2:(603)332-8090
KEENE
 THE SAMARITANS OF
  KEENE
 Crisis Phone 1:(603)357-5505

Crisis Phone 2:(603)357-5506
LEBANON
HEADREST INC.
Crisis Phone:(603)448-4400
MANCHESTER
MENTAL HEALTH CENTER
OF GREATER
MANCHESTER
Crisis Phone:(603)668-4111
PORTSMOUTH
SEACOAST MENTAL
HEALTH CENTER
Crisis Phone:(603)431-6703
SALEM
CENTER FOR LIFE
MANAGEMENT
Crisis Phone:(603)432-2253

New Jersey

ATLANTIC CITY
PSYCHIATRIC
INTERVENTION
PROGRAM ATLANTIC CITY
MEDICAL CENTER
Crisis Phone:(609)344-1118
BRIDGEWATER
GUIDELINE
Crisis Phone:(201)526-4100
CHERRY HILL
CONTACT 609, INC.
Crisis Phone 1:(609)667-3000
Crisis Phone 2:(609)428-2900
STEININGER CENTER
Crisis Phone 1:(609)428-4357
Crisis Phone 2:(609)541-2222
FLEMINGTON
HUNTERDON HELPLINE
Crisis Phone:(201)782-4357
GLASSBORO
TOGETHER, INC.
Crisis Phone:(609)881-4040
HOBOKEN
ST. MARY'S COMMUNITY
MENTAL HEALTH
Crisis Phone:(201)795-5505
LINWOOD
CONTACT ATLANTIC
COUNTY
Crisis Phone:(609)646-6616
LYNDHURST
SOUTH BERGEN MENTAL
HEALTH CENTER
Crisis Phone 1:(201)935-3322
Crisis Phone 2:(201)646-0333
MILLVILLE
MILLVILLE HOTLINE
CUMBERLAND COUNTY
GUIDANCE CENTER

Crisis Phone:(609)327-2222
MONTCLAIR
NORTH ESSEX HELP LINE
MENTAL HEALTH
RESOURCE CENTER
Crisis Phone:(201)744-1954
MOORESTOWN
CONTACT BURLINGTON
COUNTY
Crisis Phone 1:(609)234-5555
Crisis Phone 2:(609)871-4700
Crisis Phone 3:(609)267-8500
MORRISTOWN
HELPLINE
MORRISTOWN MEMORIAL
HOSPITAL
Crisis Phone:(201)540-5045
MT. HOLLY
SCREENING AND CRISIS
INTERVENTION
PROGRAM MEMORIAL
HOSPITAL OF
BURLINGTON COUNTY
Crisis Phone:(609)261-8000
NEWARK
EMERGENCY PSYCHIATRIC
SERVICES
Crisis Phone 1:(201)456-6134
Crisis Phone 2:(201)623-2323
Crisis Phone 3:(201)623-2344
Crisis Phone 4:(201)623-2345
NEWARK EMERGENCY
SERVICES
MT. CARMEL GUILD
COMMUNITY MENTAL
HEALTH CENTER
Crisis Phone:(201)596-4100
PEQUANNOCK
CONTACT MORRIS- PASSAIC
Crisis Phone:(201)831-1870
RED BANK
HELPLINE—CRISIS UNIT
RIVERVIEW MEDICAL
CENTER/CHILDREN'S
PSYCHIATRIC CENTER
MENTAL HEALTH
SERVICES
Crisis Phone:(201)671-5250
RICHWOOD
CONTACT GLOUCESTER
COUNTY
Crisis Phone:(609)881-6200
SALEM
CONTACT HELP OF SALEM
COUNTY
Crisis Phone:(609)935-4357
TOMS RIVER
CONTACT OF OCEAN
COUNTY
Crisis Phone 1:(201)240-6100
Crisis Phone 2:(609)693-5834

TRENTON
CONTACT OF MERCER
COUNTY
Crisis Phone 1:(609)896-2120
Crisis Phone 2:(609)585-2244
UNION
COMMUNICATION—HELP
CENTER KEAN COLLEGE
OF NEW JERSEY
Crisis Phone 1:(201)527-2360
Crisis Phone 2:(201)527-2330
Crisis Phone 3:(201)289-2101
WESTFIELD
CONTACT—WE CARE, INC.
Crisis Phone 1:(201)232-2880
Crisis Phone 2:(201)232-2444

New Mexico

ALBUQUERQUE
AGORA UNIVERSITY OF
NEW MEXICO CRISIS
CENTER
Crisis Phone:(505)277-3013
CONTACT LIFELINE
Crisis Phone 1:(505)293-1888
Crisis Phone 2:(505)293-1889
CRISIS UNIT BERNALILLO
COUNTY MENTAL
HEALTH CENTER
Crisis Phone:(505)843-2800
PORTALES
MENTAL HEALTH
RESOURCES, INC.
Crisis Phone:(800)432-2159

New York

ALBANY
CAPITOL DISTRICT
PSYCHIATRIC CENTER
Crisis Phone:(518)447-9650
HELPLINE
Crisis Phone:(518)436-6000
SAMARITANS OF CAPITOL
DISTRICT
Crisis Phone:(518)463-2323
BELLMORE
MIDDLE EARTH CRISIS
COUNSELING AND
REFERRAL CENTER
Crisis Phone:(516)679-1111
BUFFALO
BUFFALO SUICIDE
PREVENTION AND CRISIS
SERVICE
Crisis Phone:(716)834-3131
ELLENVILLE

FAMILY OF ELLENVILLE
Crisis Phone:(914)626-8109
GOSHEN
ORANGE COUNTY HELP
LINE MENTAL HEALTH
ASSOCIATION
Helpline:(914)343-6906
Helpline:(914)294-9355
Teenline:(914)294-9445
Helpline:(800)832-1200
Teenline:(914)565-0731
ISLIP
ISLIP HOTLINE
Crisis Phone:(516)277-4700
ITHACA
SUICIDE PREVENTION AND
CRISIS SERVICE OF
TOMPKINS COUNTY
Crisis Phone:(607)272-1616
JAMESTOWN
JAMESTOWN CRISIS LINE
JAMESTOWN GENERAL
HOSPITAL
Crisis Phone:(716)484-1314
KEENE
FAMILY COUNSELING
CENTER OF KEENE
Crisis Phone:(518)523-9720
NEW PALTZ
OASIS COUNSELING
CENTER STATE
UNIVERSITY COLLEGE
Crisis Phone:(914)257-2141
FAMILY OF NEW PALTZ
Crisis Phone:(914)255-8801
NEW YORK
HELP-LINE TELEPHONE
SERVICES
Crisis Phone:(212)532-2400
THE SAMARITANS OF NEW
YORK CITY
Crisis Phone:(212)673-3000
NIAGARA FALLS
NIAGARA HOTLINE/CRISIS
INTERVENTION SERVICE
Crisis Phone:(716)285-3515
OYSTER BAY
HARMONY HEIGHTS
SCHOOL
Crisis Phone:(516)922-1440
PEEKSKILL
PEEKSKILL CRISIS
INTERVENTION
Crisis Phone:(914)739-6403
PLATTSBURGH
PLATTSBURGH
COMMUNITY CRISIS
CENTER
Crisis Phone:(518)561-2330
POUGHKEEPSIE
DUTCHESS COUNTY

DEPARTMENT OF
MENTAL HEALTH
Crisis Phone:(914)485-9700
QUEENS VILLAGE
DIAL-FOR-HELP
CREEDMOR PSYCHIATRIC
CENTER
Crisis Phone:(718)464-7515
ROCHESTER
LIFE LINE/HEALTH
ASSOCIATION OF
ROCHESTER
Crisis Phone:(716)275-5151
STONY BROOK
RESPONSE OF SUFFOLK
COUNTY INC.
Crisis Phone:(516)751-7500
SYRACUSE
CONTACT-SYRACUSE
Crisis Phone:(315)425-1500
SUICIDE PREVENTION
SERVICE/CRISIS
COUNSELING CENTER
Crisis Phone:(315)474-1333
UTICA
UTICA CRISIS
INTERVENTION
Crisis Phone:(315)736-0883
Rome:(315)337-7299
Herkimer:(315)866-0123
VALHALLA
CRISIS INTERVENTION
UNIT WESTCHESTER
COUNTY MEDICAL
CENTER
Crisis Phone:(914)285-7075
WHITE PLAINS
MENTAL HEALTH ASSOC/
STERLING CLINIC
Suicide prevention
Service:(914)946-0121
Crisis Intervention
Service:(914)949-6741
WOODSTOCK
FAMILY OF WOODSTOCK
Crisis Phone:(914)338-2370

North Carolina

ASHVILLE
CONTACT-ASHVILLE/
BUNCOMBE
Crisis Phone:(704)253-4357
BURLINGTON
SUICIDE AND CRISIS
SERVICE/ALAMANCE
COUNTY
Crisis Phone:(919)227-6220
CHAPEL HILL

HELPLINE
Crisis Phone 1:(919)929-0479
Crisis Phone 2:(919)732-2796
Crisis Phone 3:(919)599-8366
Crisis Phone 4:(919)542-4422
Crisis Phone 5:(919)742-5612
CHARLOTTE
REACHLINE
Crisis Phone:(704)333-6121
THE RELATIVES, INC.
Crisis Phone:(704)377-0602
DURHAM
CONTACT DURHAM
Crisis Phone:(919)683-1595
Phone a Friend: (919)683-3399
HELPLINE OF DURHAM
Crisis Phone:(919)683-8628
FAYETTEVILLE
CONTACT OF
FAYETTEVILLE, INC.
Crisis Phone:(919)485-4134
FRANKLYN
RESPECT, INC.
Crisis Phone:(704)369-6143
GOLDSBORO
WAYNE COUNTY MENTAL
HEALTH CENTER
HOTLINE
Crisis Phone:(919)735-4357
GREENSBORO
CRISIS CONTROL CENTER,
INC.
Crisis Phone:(919)852-4444
SWITCHBOARD CRISIS
CENTER
Crisis Phone:(919)275-0896
GREENVILLE
REAL CRISIS
INTERVENTION, INC.
Crisis Phone 1: (919)758-HELP
Crisis Phone 2:(919)758-0787
HARRELLSVILLE
ROANOKE-CHOWAN
HUMAN SERVICES
CENTER
Crisis Phone:(919)332-4442
LEXINGTON
CONTACT DAVIDSON
COUNTY
Crisis Phone:(704)249-8974
MANTEO
OUTER BANKS HOTLINE
Crisis Phone 1:(919)473-3366
Crisis Phone 2:(919)995-5104
Crisis Phone 3:(919)338-2829
MOREHEAD
HELPLINE OF MOREHEAD
Crisis Phone:(919)247-3023
RALEIGH
HOPELINE, INC.
Crisis Phone:(919)755-6555

Teen Hopeline:(919)755-6777
ROANOKE RAPIDS
ROANOKE RAPIDS CRISIS
LINE HALIFAX COUNTY
MENTAL HEALTH
Crisis Phone:(919)537-2909
SALISBURY
SALISBURY DIAL HELP
Crisis Phone:(704)636-9222
SANFORD
LEE COUNTY MENTAL
HEALTH CRISIS LINE
Crisis Phone:(919)774-4520
SMITHFIELD
CONTACT JOHNSTON
COUNTY
Crisis Phone:(919)934-6161
STATESVILLE
THE CUP OF WATER, INC.
Crisis Phone 1:(704)872-7638
Crisis Phone 2:(704)664-4357
WILMINGTON
CRISIS LINE/OPEN HOUSE
Crisis Phone:(919)763-3695
In N.C. Only:(800)672-2903
WILSON
WILSON CRISIS CENTER
Crisis Phone:(919)237-5156
WINSTON-SALEM
CONTACT: WINSTON-
SALEM
Crisis Phone:(919)722-5153

North Dakota

BISMARCK
CRISIS AND EMERGENCY
SERVICES WEST
CENTRAL HUMAN
SERVICE CENTER
Crisis Phone:(701)255-3090
MENTAL HEALTH
ASSOCIATION OF NORTH
DAKOTA
Crisis Phone:(800)472-2911
FARGO
UNITED WAY'S HOT LINE
Crisis Phone 1:(701)235-7335
Crisis Phone 2:(701)232-4357
GRAND FORKS
NORTHEAST HUMAN
SERVICE CENTER
Crisis Phone:(701)775-0525
MINOT
MINOT SUICIDE
PREVENTION SERVICE
ST. JOSEPH'S HOSPITAL
Crisis Phone:(701)839-2222

Ohio

AKRON
SUPPORT, INC.
Crisis Phone 1:(216)434-9144
Teleteen:(216)434-9143
ASHTABULA
CONTACT ASHTABULA
Crisis Phone:(216)998-2607
ATHENS
CARELINE
Crisis Phone:(614)593-3344
BOWLING GREEN
THE LINK CRISIS CENTER
Crisis Phone 1:(419)352-1545
Crisis Phone 2:(419)352-1546
Non-Wood County: (800)472-
9411
BUCYRUS
CONTACT CRAWFORD
COUNTY
Crisis Phone 1:(419)562-9010
Crisis Phone 2:(419)468-9081
CANTON
CRISIS INTERVENTION
CENTER OF STARK
COUNTY
Crisis Phone:(216)452-6000
CHILLICOTHE
CHILLICOTHE CRISIS
CENTER SCIOTO-PAINT
VALLEY MENTAL
HEALTH CENTER
Crisis Phone:(614)773-4357
CINCINNATI
281-CARE/TALBERT HOUSE
Crisis Phone:(513)281-2273
CINCINNATI
CONTACT QUEEN CITY
Crisis Phone:(513)791-4673
CLEVELAND
CITIZENS MENTAL HEALTH
ASSEMBLY
Crisis Phone:(216)781-2944
ST. VINCENT CHARITY
HOSPITAL PSYCHIATRIC
EMERGENCY SERVICE
Crisis Phone:(216)229-2211
COLUMBUS
SUICIDE PREVENTION
SERVICES
Crisis Phone:(614)221-5445
Teen Suicide Hotline: (614)294-
3300
DAYTON
CONTACT DAYTON
Crisis Phone:(513)865-8788
SUICIDE PREVENTION
CENTER, INC.
Crisis Phone:(513)223-4777
DELAWARE

HELP ANONYMOUS, INC.
Crisis Phone 1:(614)369-3316
Crisis Phone 2:(614)548-7324
DOVER
CRISIS HELP LINE
Crisis Phone:(216)343-1811
EATON
PREBLE COUNSELING
CENTER HOTLINE
Crisis Phone:(513)456-1166
GREENVILLE
CRISIS HOTLINE DARKE
COUNTY MENTAL
HEALTH CLINIC
Crisis Phone:(513)548-1635
KENT
TOWNHALL II HELPLINE
Crisis Phone:(216)678-4357
Portage County Only: (800)533-
4357
LANCASTER
INFORMATION AND CRISIS
SERVICE/FAIRFIELD
COUNTY
Crisis Phone:(614)687-0500
MANSFIELD
HELP LINE/ADAPT
Crisis Phone:(419)522-4357
MARION
CARE LINE
Crisis Phone:(614)387-7200
MARYSVILLE
UNION COUNTY CRISIS
HOTLINE CHARLES B.
MILLS CENTER
Crisis Phone:(513)644-6363
Plain City:(614)873-8610
Richwood:(614)943-2916
MEDINA
MEDINA CRISIS
INTERVENTION HELP
LINE CATHOLIC SOCIAL
SERVICES
Crisis Phone 1:(216)725-4357
Crisis Phone 2:(216)225-4357
Crisis Phone 3:(216)336-4357
MT. GILEAD
HOPE LINE, INC.
Crisis Phone:(419)947-2520
OXFORD
OXFORD CRISIS AND
REFERRAL CENTER
Crisis Phone:(513)523-4146
PORTSMOUTH
SCIOTO COUNTY DRUG
ABUSE COUNCIL, INC.
Crisis Phone:(614)354-1010
Scioto, Adams County:(800)448-
2273
Lawrence County: (800)448-2273
TOLEDO

THE NEW RESCUE CRISIS
SERVICE
Crisis Phone:(419)255-5500
TOLEDO FIRST CALL FOR
HELP
Crisis Phone:(419)244-3728
XENIA
GREENE COUNTY CRISIS
CENTER
Crisis Phone 1:(513)429-0679
Crisis Phone 2:(513)429-0933
YOUNGSTOWN
HELP HOTLINE, INC.
Crisis Phone 1:(216)747-2696
Crisis Phone 2:(216)424-7767
Crisis Phone 3:(216)426-9355
ZANESVILLE
SIX COUNTY, INC. CRISIS
HOTLINE
Crisis Phone:(614)452-8403

Oklahoma

CLINTON
CONTACT WESTERN
OKLAHOMA
Crisis Phone:(405)323-1064
ENID
CONTACT NORTHWEST
OKLAHOMA
Crisis Phone:(405)234-1111
LAWTON
CRISIS TELEPHONE
SERVICE
Crisis Phone:(405)355-7575
OKLAHOMA CITY
CONTACT OF
METROPOLITAN
OKLAHOMA CITY
Crisis Phone:(405)848-2273
TEENLINE DEPARTMENT
OF MENTAL HEALTH
Crisis Phone 1:(405)235-3700
Crisis Phone 2: (800)522-TEEN
PONCA CITY
HELPLINE/PONCA CITY
Crisis Phone:(405)765-5551
TULSA
TULSA HELPLINE
Crisis Phone:(918)583-4357

Oregon

ALBANY
LINN COUNTY MENTAL
HEALTH
Crisis Phone:(503)757-2299
CORVALLIS

BENTON COUNTY MENTAL
HEALTH
Crisis Phone:(503)757-2299
EUGENE
MENTAL HEALTH
EMERGENCY CENTER
Crisis Phone:(503)687-4000
WHITE BIRD CLINIC
Crisis Phone 1:(503)342-8255
Crisis Phone 2:(503)687-4000
GRANTS PASS
HELPLINE REFERRAL
SERVICES
Crisis Phone:(503)479-4357
KLAMATH FALLS
KLAMATH CRISIS CENTER
Crisis Phone 1:(503)884-0636
Crisis Phone 2:(503)884-0390
MEDFORD
CRISIS INTERVENTION
SERVICES
Crisis Phone:(503)779-4357
PORTLAND
METRO CRISIS
INTERVENTION SERVICE
Crisis Phone:(503)223-6161
SALEM
NORTHWEST HUMAN
SERVICES, INC.
Crisis Phone:(503)581-5535

Pennsylvania

ABINGTON
TELEHELP OF
MONTGOMERY COUNTY
Crisis Phone:(215)884-2220
ALLENTOWN
CRISIS INTERVENTION
TEAM LEHIGH COUNTY
Crisis Phone:(215)820-3127
ALTOONA
CONTACT ALTOONA
Crisis Phone 1:(814)946-9050
CAMP HILL
TEENLINE HOLY SPIRIT
HOSPITAL, COMMUNITY
MENTAL HEALTH
CENTER
Crisis Phone 1:(800)722-5385
Crisis Phone 2:(717)763-2345
CHAMBERSBURG
CONTACT CHAMBERSBURG
Crisis Phone:(717)264-7799
DOWNINGTOWN
CRISIS INTERVENTION
(HUMAN SERVICES INC)
CHESTER COUNTY CRISIS
INTERVENTION CENTER

Crisis Phone:(215)873-1000
ERIE
INFORMATION AND
REFERRAL DIVISION
UNITED WAY OF ERIE
COUNTY
Erie Hotline:(814)453-5656
GASTON
EMERGENCY SERVICES
UNIT NORTHAMPTON
COUNTY
Crisis Phone:(215)252-9060
GETTYSBURG
ADAMS/HANOVER
COUNSELING SERVICE
9AM-5PM:(717)334-0468
After Hours:(717)334-2121
HARRISBURG
CONTACT HARRISBURG
Crisis Phone 1:(717)652-4400
Crisis Phone 2:(800)932-4616
DAUPHIN COUNTY CRISIS
INTERVENTION
Crisis Phone:(717)232-7511
INDIANA
THE OPEN DOOR
Crisis Phone:(412)465-2605
LANCASTER
CONTACT LANCASTER
Crisis Phone:(717)299-4855
Teen line:(717)394-2000
MEDIA
DELAWARE COUNTY CRISIS
INTERVENTION
Crisis Phone:(215)565-4300
NANTICOKE
HAZLETON-NANTICOKE
CRISIS SERVICES
HAZLETON-NANTICOKE
MENTAL HEALTH
CENTER
Crisis Phone 1:(717)735-7590
Crisis Phone 2:(717)455-6385
NEW BLOOMFIELD
PERRY COUNTY HOTLINE
Crisis Phone:(717)582-8052
NEW BRIGHTON
CONTACT BEAVER VALLEY
Crisis Phone:(412)728-3650
NEW CASTLE
CONTACT E.A.R.S.
Crisis Phone:(412)658-5529
NEWTOWN
CONTACT LOWER BUCKS
Crisis Phone:(215)752-1850
NORRISTOWN
MONTGOMERY COUNTY
EMERGENCY SERVICE,
INC.
Crisis Phone:(215)279-6100
PHILADELPHIA

CONTACT PHILADELPHIA
Crisis Phone:(215)879-4402
PHILADELPHIA SUICIDE
CENTER
Crisis Phone:(215)686-4420
SUICIDE AND CRISIS
INTERVENTION CENTER
Crisis Phone:(215)686-4420
SURVIVORS OF SUICIDE,
INC.
Crisis Phone:(215)545-2242
TEEN SUICIDE TREATMENT
AND PREVENTION
PROGRAM
HAHNEMANN UNIVERSITY
HOSPITAL
Crisis Phone:(215)448-4800
PITTSBURGH
CONTACT PITTSBURGH,
INC.
Crisis Phone:(412)782-4023
UNITED WAY OF
ALLEGHENY COUNTY
HELPLINE
Crisis Phone:(412)255-1155
SCRANTON
FREE INFORMATION AND
REFERRAL SYSTEM
Crisis Phone:(717)961-1234
SHARON HILL
COMMUNITY LIFE
SERVICES, INC.
Crisis Phone:(215)534-3636
SHARPSVILLE
CONTACT PENN-OHIO
Crisis Phone:(412)962-5777
WILKES-BARRE
COMMUNITY COUNSELING
SERVICES OF NORTH
EAST PENNSYLVANIA
Crisis Phone:(717)823-2155
WILLIAMSPORT
WILLIAMSPORT HELPLINE
Crisis Phone 1:(717)323-8555
Crisis Phone 2:(800)624-4636
YORK
CONTACT YORK
Crisis Phone 1:(717)845-3656
Crisis Phone 2:(717)845-9123
CRISIS INTERVENTION
SERVICES OF YORK
Crisis Phone:(717)845-2718

Rhode Island

PROVIDENCE
THE SAMARITANS OF
PROVIDENCE
Crisis Phone:(401)272-4044

WAKEFIELD
SYMPATICO
Crisis Phone:(401)783-0650

South Carolina

AIKEN
AIKEN COUNTY HELP LINE,
INC.
Crisis Phone:(803)648-9900
CHARLESTON HTS
CHARLESTON HOTLINE
Crisis Phone:(803)744-4357
Statewide:(800)922-2283
COLUMBIA
HELPLINE OF THE
MIDLANDS, INC.
Crisis Phone 1:(803)771-4357
Crisis Phone 2:(803)771-6310
CONWAY
COASTAL CAROLINA
HOSPITAL
Crisis Phone:(800)922-0742
GAFFNEY
CHEROKEE SUICIDE
INTERVENTION CENTER,
INC.
Crisis Help-line: (803)487-HELP
GREENVILLE
HELP-LINE/GREENVILLE
Crisis Phone: (803)233-HELP

South Dakota

ABERDEEN
NEW BEGINNINGS CENTER
Crisis Phone:(605)229-1239
HURON
OUR HOME, INC.
Crisis Phone:(605)352-9449
SIOUX FALLS
CRISIS LINE/SIOUX FALLS
VOLUNTEER AND
INFORMATION CENTER
Crisis Phone:(605)339-4357
HELPLINE OF SIOUX FALLS
Crisis Phone:(605)339-4357

Tennessee

ATHENS
MC MINN/MEIGS CONTACT
Crisis Phone:(615)745-9111
CHATTANOOGA
CONTACT OF
CHATTANOOGA

Crisis Phone 1:(615)266-8228
Crisis Phone 2:(615)622-5193
CLEVELAND
CLEVELAND HELPLINE
Crisis Phone:(615)479-9666
JOHNSON CITY
CONTACT MINISTRIES
Crisis Phone:(615)926-0144
KINGSPORT
CONTACT—CONCERN
Crisis Phone:(615)246-2273
KNOXVILLE
CONTACT TELEPHONE OF
KNOXVILLE
Crisis Phone:(615)523-9124
HELEN ROSS MC NABB
CENTER
Crisis Phone:(615)637-9711
MARYVILLE
CONTACT OF BLOUNT
COUNTY
Crisis Phone:(615)984-7689
CONTACT TELEMINISTRIES
OF BLOUNT COUNTY
Crisis Phone:(615)984-7689
MEMPHIS
CHARTER LAKESIDE
HOSPITAL
Crisis Phone:(901)377-4733
SUICIDE/CRISIS
INTERVENTION SERVICE/
MEMPHIS
Crisis Phone:(901)274-7477
NASHVILLE
CRISIS INTERVENTION
CENTER, INC.
Crisis Phone:(615)244-7444
OAK RIDGE
CONTACT OF OAK RIDGE
Crisis Phone:(615)482-4949
TULLAHOMA
TULLAHOMA CONTACT—
LIFE LINE
Coffee County:(615)455-7133
Franklin County: (615)967-7133
Bedford County: (615)684-7133
Moore County: (615)759-7133

Texas

AMARILLO
SUICIDE AND CRISIS
CENTER
Crisis Phone:(806)359-6699
Toll-free In-state: (800)692-4039
ARLINGTON
CONTACT TARRANT
COUNTY
Crisis Phone:(817)277-2233

AUSTIN
AUSTIN-TRAVIS COUNTY
MENTAL HEALTH
CENTER
Crisis Phone: (512)472-HELP
INFORMATION HOTLINE
AND CRISIS CENTER
Crisis Phone: (512)472-HELP
BEAUMONT
RAPE AND SUICIDE CRISIS
OF SE TEXAS
Crisis Phone:(409)835-3355
SUICIDE RESCUE, INC.
Crisis Phone:(713)833-2311
CORPUS CHRISTI
CRISIS SERVICES/CORPUS
CHRISTI
Crisis Phone:(512)993-7410
DALLAS
CONTACT-DALLAS/
TELEPHONE
COUNSELING
Crisis Phone:(214)233-2233
Teen-contact: (214)233-TEEN
SUICIDE AND CRISIS
CENTER
Crisis Phone:(214)828-1000
DEL RIO
DEL RIO CRISIS LINE
YOUTH COUSELING
CENTER
Crisis Phone:(512)775-0571
EL PASO
EL PASO CRISIS
INTERVENTION
SERVICES
Crisis Phone:(915)779-1800
FORT WORTH
CRISIS INTERVENTION
Crisis Phone:(817)927-5544
HOUSTON
CRISIS INTERVENTION OF
HOUSTON, INC.
Central:(713)228-1505
Bay Area:(713)333-5111
HARRIS COUNTY
PSYCHIATRIC
INTERVENTION
DEPARTMENT OF MENTAL
HEALTH
Crisis Phone:(713)741-6000
HOUSTON-BAY AREA CRISIS
HELPLINE
Crisis Phone:(713)333-5111
RX FOR CRISIS
Crisis Phone 1:(713)795-4878
Crisis Phone 2:(713)795-4511
LAREDO
LIFELINE OF LAREDO, INC.
Crisis Phone:(512)722-5433
LUBBOCK

CONTACT LUBBOCK
Crisis Phone:(806)765-8393
Teen Line:(806)765-7272
ORANGE
SUICIDE RESCUE
Crisis Phone:(713)883-5521
PLANO
CRISIS CENTER OF COLLIN
COUNTY
Crisis Phone 1:(214)881-0088
Crisis Phone 2:(214)542-8500
RICHARDSON
RICHARDSON CRISIS
CENTER
Crisis Phone:(214)783-0008
SAN ANGELO
CONCHO VALLEY CENTER
FOR HUMAN ADVANCE
Crisis Phone:(915)653-5933
SAN ANTONIO
CONTACT SAN ANTONIO
Crisis Phone:(512)733-1111
VICTORIA
HOPE OF SOUTH TEXAS
Crisis Phone:(512)573-3600
WICHITA FALLS
CONCERN, INC.
Crisis Phone:(817)723-0821

Utah

LOGAN
LOGAN HELPLINE
Crisis Phone:(801)752-3964
MIDVALE
SALT LAKE COUNTY
DIVISION OF MENTAL
HEALTH
Crisis Phone:(801)566-2455
OGDEN
OGDEN EMERGENCY
SERVICES WEBER
COUNTY MENTAL
HEALTH CENTER
Crisis Phone:(801)626-9270
PROVO
UTAH COUNTY CRISIS LINE
Crisis Phone:(801)377-8259
SALT LAKE CITY
SALT LAKE CITY CRISIS
INTERVENTION
Crisis Phone:(801)581-2296
SALT LAKE VALLEY
MENTAL HEALTH
Crisis Phone:(801)483-5444

Vermont

BRATTLEBORO
HOTLINE FOR HELP, INC.

Crisis Phone:(802)257-7989
BURLINGTON
THE CRISIS SERVICES OF
CHITTENDEN COUNTY
Crisis Phone:(802)656-3587
RANDOLPH
ORANGE COUNTY MENTAL
HEALTH SERVICE
EMERGENCY SERVICE
Crisis Phone:(800)622-4244
ST. ALBANS
ST. ALBANS EMERGENCY
AND CRISIS SERVICE
FRANKLIN GRAND ISLE
MENTAL HEALTH
SERVICE, INC.
Crisis Phone:(802)524-6554

Virginia

ALEXANDRIA
ALEXANDRIA C.A.I.R.
HOTLINE
Crisis Phone:(703)548-3810
ALEXANDRIA COMMUNITY
MENTAL HEALTH
CENTER
Crisis Phone:(703)836-5751
ARLINGTON
NORTHERN VIRGINIA
HOTLINE
Crisis Phone:(703)527-4077
BLACKSBURG
RAFT COMMUNITY CRISIS
CENTER
Crisis Phone:(703)382-1738
BRISTOL
BRISTOL CRISIS CENTER
Crisis Phone 1:(703)466-2312
Crisis Phone 2:(703)628-7731
FREDERICKSBURG
FREDERICKSBURG
HOTLINE
Crisis Phone:(703)321-1212
HARRISONBURG
LISTENING EAR SERVICES
MASSANUTTEN MENTAL
HEALTH CENTER
Crisis Phone:(703)434-2538
LYNCHBURG
THE CRISIS LINE OF
CENTRAL VIRGINIA
Crisis Phone:(804)528-help
MANASSA
COMMUNITY MENTAL
HEALTH
Crisis Phone:(703)361-3101
MARTINSVILLE
CONTACT MARTINSVILLE-
HENRY COUNTY

Crisis Phone:(703)632-7295
PETERSBURG
CONTACT OLD DOMINION,
INC.
Petersburg:(804)733-1100
Can Help/Richmond:(804)226-4357
Statewide:(800)768-CARE
PORTSMOUTH
SUICIDE-CRISIS CENTER,
INC.
Crisis Phone:(804)399-6393
RICHMOND
CONTACT OLD
DOMINION—RICHMOND
Crisis Phone:(804)226-4357
CRISIS INTERVENTION
(RICHMOND)
RICHMOND COMMUNITY
MENTAL HEALTH
CENTER
Crisis Phone 1:(804)780-8003
Crisis Phone 2:(804)648-9224
ROANOKE
SANCTUARY
Crisis Phone:(703)981-2776
TRUST: ROANOKE VALLEY
TROUBLE CENTER
Crisis Phone 1:(703)344-1978
Crisis Phone 2:(703)344-1948
VIRGINIA BEACH
CONTACT TIDEWATER
Crisis Phone:(804)428-2211
WINCHESTER
CONCERN HOTLINE, INC.
Winchester:(703)667-0145
Front Royal:(703)635-4357
Woodstock:(703)459-4742

Washington

B'BRIDGE ISLAND
HELPLINE HOUSE
Crisis Phone: (206)842-HELP
BELLINGHAM
THE CRISIS LINE
WHATCOM COUNTY
CRISIS SERVICES
Crisis Phone 1:(206)734-7271
Whatcom County: (206)384-1485
BREMERTON
BREMERTON CRISIS CLINIC
Crisis Phone:(206)479-3033
CHEHALIS
LEWIS COUNTY HOTLINE &
C.A.R.E. SERVICE
Crisis Phone:(206)748-6601
In Washington: (800)458-3080
ELLENSBURG
ELLENSBURG CRISIS LINE

Crisis Phone:(509)925-4168
EVERETT
CARE CRISIS LINE
Crisis Phone:(206)258-4357
MOSES LAKE
GRANT COUNTY CRISIS
LINE MENTAL HEALTH
AND FAMILY SERVICE
Crisis Phone:(509)765-1717
OLYMPIA
CRISIS CLINIC
Thurston County: (206)352-2211
Mason County: (206)426-3311
PULLMAN
WHITMAN COUNTY CRISIS
LINE/LATAH COUNTY
NIGHTLINE
Crisis Phone:(509)332-1505
RICHLAND
CONTACT TRI-CITIES AREA
Crisis Phone:(509)943-6606
SEATTLE
CRISIS CLINIC
Crisis Phone:(206)461-3222
SPOKANE
CRISIS HOTLINE/SPOKANE
SPOKANE COMMUNITY
MENTAL HEALTH
CENTER
Crisis Phone:(509)838-4428
TACOMA
LIFELINE INSTITUTE FOR
SUICIDE PREVENTION
Crisis Phone 1:(206)584-3733
Crisis Phone 2:(206)584-3735
TACOMA CRISIS LINE
Crisis Phone:(206)759-6700
YAKIMA
OPEN LINE/YAKIMA
CENTRAL WASHINGTON
COMPREHENSIVE
MENTAL HEALTH
Crisis Phone:(509)575-4200
Statewide Toll-free: (800)572-8122

West Virginia

CHARLESTON
CONTACT KANAWHA
VALLEY CHRIST CHURCH
UNITED METHODIST
Crisis Phone:(304)346-0826
HUNTINGTON
CONTACT HUNTINGTON
Crisis Phone:(304)523-3448
PRESTERA CENTER FOR
MENTAL HEALTH
SERVICES
Crisis Phone:(304)525-7851

LEWISBURG
GREENBRIAR VALLEY
MENTAL HEALTH CLINIC
Crisis Phone:(304)647-5587
PRINCETON
SOUTHERN HIGHLANDS
COMMUNITY MENTAL
HEALTH CENTER
Crisis Phone:(304)425-9541
WHEELING
UPPER OHIO VALLEY
CRISIS HOTLINE
Crisis Phone:(304)234-8161

Wisconsin

APPLETON
APPLETON CRISIS
INTERVENTION CENTER
Crisis Phone:(414)731-3211
LIFE LINE/APPLETON
Crisis Phone:(414)734-2323
BELOIT
BELOIT HOTLINE
STATELINE AREA YWCA
Crisis Phone:(608)365-4436
CEDARBURG
COPE OZAUKEE COUNTY
HOTLINE
Crisis Phone:(414)377-2673
EAU CLAIRE
SUICIDE PREVENTION
CENTER
Crisis Phone:(715)834-6040
ELKHORN
LAKELAND COUNSELING
CENTER
Crisis Phone:(414)741-3200
FOND DU LAC
CIC/FOND DU LAC
Crisis Phone:(414)929-3535
GREEN BAY
CRISIS INTERVENTION
CENTER/GREEN BAY
Crisis Phone:(414)432-8832
LA CROSSE
FIRST CALL FOR HELP (LA
CROSSE)
First Call For Help: (608)782-8010
First Call Wisconsin:(800)362-8255
First Call Minnesota &
Iowa:(800)356-9588
HARBOR HOUSE
Crisis Phone:(608)785-0530
MADISON
EMERGENCY SERVICES
MENTAL HEALTH
CENTER OF DANE

COUNTY, INC.
Crisis Phone:(608)251-2345
MULWAUKEE
SURVIVORS HELPING
SURVIVORS
ST. LUKE'S MEDICAL
CENTER
Crisis Phone 1:(414)649-6000
Crisis Phone 2:(414)649-6230
UNDERGROUND
SWITCHBOARD
Crisis Phone:(414)271-3123

STURGEON BAY
HELPLINE-HELP OF DOOR
COUNTY, INC.
Crisis Phone:(414)743-8818
WISCONSIN RAPIDS
WOOD COUNTY UNIFIED
SERVICES CRISIS
INTERVENTION AND
REFERRAL
Wisconsin Rapids: (715)421-2345
Marshfield:(715)384-5555

Wyoming

CHEYENNE
CHEYENNE HELPLINE
Crisis Phone:(307)634-4469
WORLAND
COMMUNITY CRISIS
SERVICE, INC.
Crisis Phone:(307)347-4991

Bibliography

Alvarez, Alfred. *The Savage God: A Study of Suicide.* New York: Banton Books, 1973.

Barrett, Tom. *Youth in Crisis.* Longmont, CO: Sopris West, 1985.

Bolton, Iris. *My Son, My Son.* Atlanta: Bolton Press, 1983.

Cain, Albert C., ed. *Survivors of Suicide.* Springfield IL: Charles C. Thomas, 1972.

Capuzzi, Ware, and Golden, Harry. *Preventing Adolescent Suicide.* Muncie, IN: Accelarated Development, 1988.

Colgrove, Melba, Bloomfield, Harold H., and McWilliams, Peter. *How to Survive the Loss of a Love.* Toronto: Bantam Books, 1976.

Davis, Patricia A. *Suicidal Adolescents.* Springfield IL: Charles C. Thomas, 1983.

Dunne, E., McIntosh, & Dunne-Maxim, K. *Suicide and Its Aftermath.* New York: W. W. Norton, 1986.

Elkind, David. *All Grown Up & No Place to Go: Teenagers in Crisis.* Reading, MA: Addison-Wesley, 1984.

Finch, J.M. and Poznanski, E.D. *Adolescent Suicide.* Springfield: Charles C. Thomas, 1971.

Giovacchine, Peter. *The Urge to Die. Why Young People Kill Themselves.* New York: Macmillan, 1981.

Gordon, Sol. *When Living Hurts.* New York: Yad Tikvah, 1985.

Griffin, M. & Felsenthal, C. *A Cry for Help.* New York: Doubleday, 1983.

Grollman, Earl. *Suicide: Prevention, Intervention, Postvention.* Boston: Beacon Press, 1971.

Haim, Andre. *Adolescent Suicide.* New York: International University Press, 1974.

Hendin, Herbert. *Suicide in America.* New York: W.W. Norton, 1982.

Husian, S. & Vandiver, T. *Suicide in Children and Adolescents.* New York: Special Medical and Scientific Books, 1984.

Hewett, John H. *After Suicide.* Philadelphia: Westminster Press, 1980.

Jacobs, Jerry. *Adolescent Suicide.* New York: Wiley-Interscience, 1974.

Joan, Polly. *Preventing Teen Age Suicide.* New York: Human Sciences Press, 1986.

Klagsbrun, Francine. *Too Young to Die.* Boston: Houghton Mifflin, 1981.

Mack, J.E. & Hickler, H. *Vivienne: The Life and Suicide of a Young Girl.* New York: The New Library, 1981.

Madison, Arnold. *Suicide and Young People.* New York: Houghton Mifflin, 1978.

McIntire, M. & Angle, C. *Suicide Attempts in Children and Youth.* Cambridge: Harper and Row, 1980.

Peck, M., Farberow, N., & Litman, R. *Youth Suicide.* New York: Springer, 1985.

Pfeffer, Cynthia. *The Suicidal Child.* New York: Guilford, 1986.

Rabkin, Brenda. *Growing Up Dead: A Hard Look at Why Adolescents Commit Suicide.* Nashville: Abingdon, 1983.

Shneidman, Edwin. *Definition of Suicide.* New York: Wiley-Interscience, 1985.

Shneidman, Edwin. *On the Nature of Suicide.* San Francisco: Jossey-Bass, 1973.

Schneidman, Edwin. ed. *Death and the College Student.* New York: Behavioral Publications, 1972.

Smith, Judie. *Suicide Prevention: A Crisis Curriculum for Teens and Young Adults.* Holmes Beach, Florida: Learning Publications, 1988.

Sudak, H., Ford, A., & Rushforth, N. *Suicide in the Young.* Boston: John Wright, 1984.

Wells, C.F. & Stuart, I.R. *Self-Destructive Behavior in Children and Adolescents.* New York: Van Nostrand Reinhold, 1981.

Westberg, Granger. *Good Grief.* Philadelphia: Fortress Press, 1962.

Index